PYTHON FOR DATA SCIENCE AND MACHINE LEARNING

Essential Tools for Working with Data

Moustafa Elgezery

To my family, who have always supported and encouraged me to pursue my dreams. Without their love and unwavering support, this book would not have been possible.

"Data is the new oil. It's valuable, but if unrefined it cannot really be used. It has to be changed into gas, plastic, chemicals, etc to create a valuable entity that drives profitable activity; so must data be broken down, analyzed for it to have value."

CLIVE HUMBY, MATHEMATICIAN AND DATA SCIENTIST.

CONTENTS

PREFACE

Data science and machine learning are two rapidly growing fields with a vast range of applications. From predicting customer behavior to image recognition, data science and machine learning can help us solve complex problems and make better decisions. Python, with its simplicity, flexibility, and strong community support, has become the go-to language for data science and machine learning.

This book is designed to provide a comprehensive introduction to Python and its essential libraries for data science and machine learning. It is intended for anyone who wants to learn how to use Python for data analysis, machine learning, and predictive modeling. Whether you are a student, a data analyst, a software developer, or a business analyst, this book will provide you with the essential tools and techniques needed to work with data using Python.

The book is organized into five chapters. Chapter I provides an introduction to Python and its essential libraries, including NumPy, Pandas, and Matplotlib. Chapter II covers data visualization and exploratory data analysis with Matplotlib and Seaborn. Chapter III covers supervised learning with Scikit-learn, including linear regression, logistic regression, decision trees, random forests, support vector machines, and k-nearest neighbors. Chapter IV covers unsupervised learning with Scikit-learn, including clustering with k-means and hierarchical clustering, and dimensionality reduction with principal component analysis and t-SNE. Finally, Chapter V covers deep learning with TensorFlow and Keras.

Throughout the book, you will learn by example. Each chapter includes hands-on exercises and real-world projects that demonstrate how to apply the concepts and techniques covered in the chapter to real-world problems. By the end of the book, you will have a solid foundation in Python, its essential libraries for data science and machine learning, and the ability to build and evaluate predictive models using Python.

I hope this book will be a useful resource for anyone interested in data science and machine learning. Please feel free to contact me with any feedback, suggestions, or questions you may have.

Happy coding!

Moustafa Elgezery

PROLOGUE

The Rise of Data Science and Machine Learning!

In recent years, data has become one of the most valuable commodities in the world. From small businesses to multinational corporations, organizations of all sizes are looking for ways to extract insights from the vast amounts of data they collect. This has led to the rise of two related fields: data science and machine learning.

Data science is the practice of using statistical and computational techniques to extract insights from data. It involves a wide range of skills, including programming, statistics, and data visualization. Machine learning is a subset of data science that involves using algorithms to automatically learn patterns in data.

Together, data science and machine learning are transforming the way we do business, conduct research, and understand the world around us. They have applications in fields as diverse as finance, healthcare, and social media.

Python is one of the most popular programming languages for data science and machine learning. Its simplicity, flexibility, and vast array of libraries make it an ideal tool for working with data. In this book, we will explore the essential tools and techniques you need to know to become proficient in data science and machine learning with Python.

CONTACTING ME!

You can reach me at moustafa.elgezery@outlook.com Please include the title of the book in the subject of your email.

I. GETTING STARTED WITH PYTHON AND ITS DATA SCIENCE LIBRARIES

Python is a powerful and versatile programming language that has become increasingly popular in the field of data science. With its easy-to-read syntax and a vast array of libraries, Python makes it easy to work with and manipulate large datasets, build machine learning models, and create insightful visualizations. In this chapter, we will cover the basics of Python programming and introduce some of the most popular data science libraries, including NumPy, Pandas, and Matplotlib. Whether you're a beginner or an experienced programmer, this chapter will provide you with the tools and knowledge you need to get started with Python for data science.

I.I What is Python?

Python is a popular high-level programming language that is used by developers, data scientists, and researchers around the world. With its easy-to-read syntax and powerful libraries, Python has become a go-to language for a variety of applications, including web development, data analysis, machine learning, and scientific computing. In this article, we will explore what Python is, its history, features, and applications.

What is Python?

Python is a general-purpose, high-level programming language that is designed to be easy to read and write. It was created by Guido van Rossum in the late 1980s and was first released in 1991. Since then, it has become one of the most popular programming languages in the world, thanks to its versatility and ease of use.

Features of Python

Python is known for its simplicity, ease of use, and readability. Some of the key features of Python include:

Easy-to-read syntax

Python's syntax is designed to be easy to read and understand, making it a popular language for beginners. Unlike other programming languages that use complex syntax, Python uses simple, English-like statements that make it easy to learn and use.

Interpreted language

Python is an interpreted language, which means that you don't need to compile your code before running it. This makes it faster to develop and test code, and it also makes it easier to write code that works across different platforms.

Object-oriented

Python is an object-oriented programming language, which means that it allows you to create reusable code that can be easily extended and modified. This makes it a popular choice for building large, complex applications.

Large standard library

Python comes with a large standard library that includes modules for everything from web development to data analysis. This makes it easy to get started with Python and reduces the need for developers to write code from scratch.

Applications of Python

Python is a versatile language that can be used for a wide variety of applications, including:

Web development

Python can be used to create web applications using frameworks like Django and Flask. These frameworks provide developers with everything they need to create powerful, scalable web applications.

Data analysis

Python's powerful libraries like NumPy, Pandas, and Matplotlib make it a popular choice for data analysis and visualization. These libraries make it easy to work with large datasets and create insightful visualizations.

Machine learning

Python is also a popular language for machine learning and artificial intelligence applications. Libraries like TensorFlow, Keras, and PyTorch provide developers with the tools they need to build and train machine learning models.

Scientific computing

Python is widely used in scientific computing for tasks like simulations, numerical analysis, and computational modeling. Its ease of use and powerful libraries make it a popular choice for researchers and scientists.

Conclusion

Python is a powerful and versatile programming language that is used by developers, data scientists, and researchers around the world. Its simplicity, ease of use, and powerful libraries make it a popular choice for a wide variety of applications. Whether you're a beginner or an experienced programmer, Python is a great language to learn and use.

I.II Why Python is a popular language for data science and machine learning

Python has become one of the most popular languages for data science and machine learning. With its powerful libraries and easy-to-read syntax, Python makes it easy to work with and manipulate large datasets, build machine learning models, and create insightful visualizations. In this article, we will explore why Python has become a go-to language for data scientists and machine learning engineers.

Easy-to-read syntax

Python's syntax is designed to be easy to read and understand. This makes it a popular language for beginners who are just starting to learn data science or machine learning. Unlike other programming languages that use complex syntax, Python uses simple, English-like statements that make it easy to learn and use.

Powerful libraries

Python comes with a variety of powerful libraries that are specifically designed for data science and machine learning. Some of the most popular libraries include:

NumPy

NumPy is a library for working with arrays of data. It provides fast, efficient computation of arrays and is a fundamental library for scientific computing in Python.

Pandas

Pandas is a library for working with data frames, which are similar to tables in a database. It provides powerful data manipulation tools and is a popular choice for data analysis.

Matplotlib

Matplotlib is a library for creating visualizations in Python. It provides a wide range of charts and plots for visualizing data.

Scikit-learn

Scikit-learn is a library for building machine-learning models. It provides a wide range of algorithms for classification, regression, and clustering, as well as tools for data preprocessing and model selection.

TensorFlow

TensorFlow is a library for building deep-learning models. It provides a flexible and powerful platform for building neural networks and is a popular choice for building image recognition and natural language processing models.

Interoperability

Python is a popular language for data science and machine learning because it is interoperable with other languages and tools. For example, Python can be used with SQL databases like MySQL or SectiongreSQL, and it can also be used with other programming languages like Java and C++. This makes it easy to integrate Python into existing workflows and to leverage other tools and technologies alongside Python.

Community support

Python has a large and active community of developers and users. This community has created a vast ecosystem of libraries and tools for data science and machine learning, and there are many online resources available for learning and using Python. This makes it easy to find help when you need it and to stay up-to-date with the latest developments in the field.

Conclusion

Python has become a go-to language for data science and machine learning thanks to its easy-to-read syntax, powerful libraries, interoperability, and strong community support. Whether you're a beginner or an experienced data scientist or a machine learning engineer, Python is a great language to learn and use. Its versatility and flexibility make it a powerful tool for tackling a wide range of data-related problems, from data analysis to machine learning model building.

I.III Setting up the Python environment

Python is a popular programming language used for a wide range of applications, from web development to machine learning. Setting up a Python environment is an important first step in developing Python applications. In this article, we'll go through the steps of setting up a Python environment and configuring it for your specific needs.

Installing Python

The first step in setting up a Python environment is to install Python itself. Python can be downloaded from the official Python website (https://www.python.org/downloads/). When choosing a version of Python to install, it's important to consider the requirements of any libraries or frameworks you plan to use. In general, it's recommended to use the latest version of Python, which as of this writing is Python 3.11.2.

Managing packages with pip

Once Python is installed, the next step is to install any necessary packages or libraries. Python's package manager, pip, makes it easy to install, upgrade, and manage packages. Pip comes pre-installed with Python 3.4 and later versions. To install a package, simply open a terminal or command prompt and type:

```
$ pip install package-name
```

For example, to install NumPy, a popular library for scientific computing, you would type:

```
$ pip install numpy
```

Pip can also be used to upgrade or uninstall packages:

```
$ pip install --upgrade package-name
$ pip uninstall package-name
```

Using virtual environments

One challenge of managing Python environments is ensuring that different projects have access to the packages and libraries they need without interfering with each other. One solution to this problem is to use virtual environments. Virtual environments allow you to create isolated Python environments with their installed packages and dependencies.

To create a virtual environment, open a terminal or command prompt and navigate to the directory where you want to create the environment. Then run the following command:

```
$ python -m venv environment-name
```

This will create a new virtual environment with the specified name. To activate the environment, run:

```
$ source environment-name/bin/activate
```

On Windows, the activate command is slightly different:

```
environment-name\Scripts\activate.bat
```

Once activated, any packages installed with pip will be installed within the virtual environment, rather than globally on your system. This allows you to manage dependencies and package versions on a per-project basis.

Configuring your environment

Finally, you may want to configure your Python environment to suit your specific needs. This can include setting environment variables, configuring your editor or IDE, or setting up debugging and testing tools.

Some popular tools for configuring Python environments include:

- **PyCharm:** an IDE with built-in support for virtual environments, debugging, and testing.

- **VSCode:** a popular editor with a wide range of Python extensions and plugins.

- **Anaconda:** a distribution of Python that includes many popular data science and scientific computing libraries.

- **Google Colab:** is a free Jupyter Notebook environment that runs entirely in Google Cloud. It has many libraries already installed to manipulate data and train Machine Learning models, even using the cloud machine's GPU.

Conclusion

Setting up a Python environment is an important first step in developing Python applications. By installing Python, managing packages with pip, using virtual environments, and configuring your environment to suit your needs, you can create a powerful and flexible environment for building Python applications. With the right tools and setup, Python can be a powerful language for a wide range of applications, from web development to machine learning.

I.IV Using the Jupyter notebook and Google Colab

The Jupyter notebook is a popular interactive computing environment that allows you to create and share documents that contain live code, equations, visualizations, and narrative text. Google Colab is a free online platform that provides access to a Jupyter notebook environment hosted on Google's servers. In this article, we'll go through the basics of using Jupyter notebooks and Google Colab for data analysis and scientific computing.

Getting started with Jupyter notebooks

To use Jupyter notebooks, you first need to install the Jupyter software. The easiest way to do this is to install the Anaconda distribution of Python, which comes with Jupyter pre-installed. Anaconda is available for Windows, macOS, and Linux and can be downloaded from the Anaconda website (https://www.anaconda.com/products/individual).

Once you have Anaconda installed, you can launch the Jupyter notebook interface by opening a terminal or command prompt and typing:

```
$ jupyter notebook
```

This will launch a web browser with the Jupyter notebook interface. From here, you can create a new notebook or open an existing one.

Using Google Colab

Google Colab is a free online platform that provides access to a Jupyter notebook environment hosted on Google's servers. To use Google Colab, you first need a Google account. Once you have a Google account, you can access Google Colab by going to the Google Colab website (https://colab.research.google.com/).

Google Colab allows you to create and run Jupyter notebooks in the cloud, which means that you can run code on powerful servers without needing to install any software on your local machine. You can also share your notebooks with others and collaborate in real-time.

Creating a notebook

To create a new notebook in Jupyter or Google Colab, simply click the "New" button and select "Python 3" or another programming language of your choice. This will create a new notebook with an empty cell where you can enter the code.

Jupyter notebooks are organized into cells, which can contain code, text, or visualizations. To execute a cell, simply click the "Run" button or press Shift+Enter.

Importing libraries

One of the advantages of using Jupyter notebooks or Google Colab is that they make it easy to import and use external libraries, such as NumPy, Pandas, and Matplotlib. To import a library, simply type:

```
import library_name
```

For example, to import NumPy, you would type:

```
import numpy as np
```

This creates a namespace alias for the NumPy library, which allows you to refer to NumPy functions and objects using the shorthand "np".

Visualizing data

Jupyter notebooks and Google Colab make it easy to create

visualizations of data using libraries such as Matplotlib and Seaborn. To create a plot, simply import the library and use its functions to create a visualization.

For example, to create a line plot using Matplotlib, you would type:

```
import numpy as np
import matplotlib.pyplot as plt
x = np.linspace(0, 10, 100)
y = np.sin(x)
plt.plot(x, y)
plt.show()
```

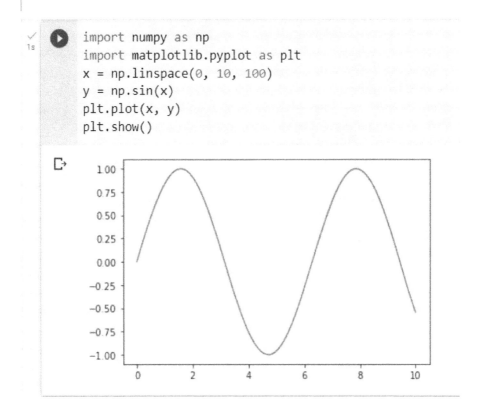

This code creates a line plot of the sine function using Matplotlib.

Conclusion

Jupyter notebooks and Google Colab are powerful tools for data analysis and scientific computing. By providing an interactive computing environment that combines code, text, and visualizations, they make it easy to explore data and communicate results. Whether you're a data scientist, a student, or an enthusiast, Jupyter notebooks and Google Colab are valuable tools to have in your toolkit.

I.V Python Data types and Operators

Python is a popular programming language that offers a variety of data types and operators to manipulate them. In this article, we'll explore some of the most commonly used data types in Python and the operators that can be used to manipulate them.

Numeric Data Types

Numeric data types are used to represent numerical values. There are three main numeric data types in Python: integers, floating-point numbers, and complex numbers.

Integers

Integers, also known as ints, are whole numbers without a fractional component. They can be positive or negative, and they have no limit on their size. In Python, you can create an integer by simply assigning a whole number to a variable. For example:

```
x = 5
```

Floating-Point Numbers

Floating-point numbers, also known as floats, are numbers with a decimal point. They can be positive or negative, and they can have a fractional component. In Python, you can create a float by simply assigning a number with a decimal point to a variable. For example:

```
y = 3.14
```

Complex Numbers

Complex numbers are numbers with real and imaginary

components. In Python, you can create a complex number by adding a "j" or "J" suffix to the imaginary part of the number. For example:

```
z = 2 + 3j
```

String Data Type

A string is a sequence of characters. In Python, you can create a string by enclosing a sequence of characters in single quotes, double quotes, or triple quotes. For example:

```
name = 'John'
```

Strings are immutable, which means that once you create a string, you cannot change its contents. However, you can manipulate strings using various string methods and operators.

Boolean Data Type

A Boolean data type is used to represent truth values. There are two Boolean values in Python: True and False. Boolean values are often used in conditional statements and loops to control the flow of a program.

Operators

Operators are used to manipulating data types in Python. There are several types of operators in Python, including arithmetic operators, comparison operators, logical operators, and bitwise operators.

Arithmetic Operators

Arithmetic operators are used to performing arithmetic operations on numeric data types. The most commonly used arithmetic operators in Python are:

- Addition: **+**
- Subtraction: **-**
- Multiplication: *****
- Division: **/**
- Modulus: **%**
- Exponentiation: ******
- Floor division: **//**

Comparison Operators

Comparison operators are used to comparing two values and return a Boolean value. The most commonly used comparison operators in Python are:

- Equal to: **==**
- Not equal to: **!=**
- Greater than: **>**
- Less than: **<**
- Greater than or equal: **>=**
- Less than or equal: **<=**

Logical Operators

Logical operators are used to combining two or more Boolean values and return a Boolean value. The most commonly used logical operators in Python are:

- And: **and**
- Or: **or**
- Not: **not**

Bitwise Operators

Bitwise operators are used to performing bitwise operations on integer values. The most commonly used bitwise operators in Python are:

- Bitwise AND: **&**
- Bitwise OR: |
- Bitwise XOR: ^
- Bitwise NOT: ~
- Left shift: <<
- Right shift: >>

Conclusion

Python offers a variety of data types and operators to manipulate them. By understanding these data types and operators, you can write more efficient and expressive Python code. Whether you're a beginner

I.VI Python Data structures

Python is a popular programming language that provides a variety of data structures to store and manipulate data. In this article, we'll explore some of the most commonly used data structures in Python and how to use them.

Lists

Lists are one of the most commonly used data structures in Python. A list is an ordered collection of items, and each item can be of any data type. In Python, you can create a list by enclosing a sequence of items in square brackets, separated by commas. For example:

```
my_list = [1, 2, 3, 'four', 5.0]
```

Lists are mutable, which means that you can add, remove, or modify items after the list is created. You can access individual items in a list by their index, which starts at 0. For example, to access the first item in the list above, you would use:

```
print(my_list[0])
```

Lists also support a variety of built-in methods for manipulating and accessing their contents, such as **append()**, **remove()**, and **sort()**.

Tuples

Tuples are similar to lists in that they are ordered collections of items, but they are immutable, which means that you cannot modify their contents once they are created. In Python, you can create a tuple by enclosing a sequence of items in parentheses, separated by commas. For example:

```
my_tuple = (1, 2, 3, 'four', 5.0)
```

You can access individual items in a tuple by their index, just like in a list. Tuples also supports a variety of built-in methods for manipulating and accessing their contents, such as **count()** and **index()**.

Sets

Sets are unordered collections of unique items. In Python, you can create a set by enclosing a sequence of items in curly braces, separated by commas, or by using the built-in **set()** function. For example:

```
my_set = {1, 2, 3, 'four', 5.0}
```

Sets do not support indexing, but they support a variety of built-in methods for manipulating and accessing their contents, such as **add()**, **remove()**, and **union()**.

Dictionaries

Dictionaries are unordered collections of key-value pairs. In Python, you can create a dictionary by enclosing a sequence of key-value pairs in curly braces, separated by colons, or by using the built-in **dict()** function. For example:

```
my_dict = {'name': 'John', 'age': 30, 'gender': 'male'}
```

You can access individual values in a dictionary by their keys, like this:

```
print(my_dict['name'])
```

Dictionaries also support a variety of built-in methods for manipulating and accessing their contents, such as **keys()**, **values()**, and **items()**.

Conclusion

Python provides a variety of data structures to store and manipulate data. By understanding these data structures and their built-in methods, you can write more efficient and expressive Python code. Whether you're a beginner or an experienced Python developer, knowing when to use each data structure can help you write more effective programs.

I.VII Python Control flow

Python control flow refers to the order in which statements are executed in a Python program. In this article, we'll explore the various control flow statements in Python and how to use them.

Conditional Statements

Conditional statements allow you to control the flow of your program based on certain conditions. The most common conditional statement in Python is the **if** statement, which allows you to execute a block of code only if a certain condition is true. For example:

```
x = 5
if x > 3:
  print("x is greater than 3")
```

In this example, the **if** statement checks whether the value of **x** is greater than 3, and if it is, it executes the **print()** statement.

You can also use the **if** statement in combination with the **else** statement to execute a different block of code if the condition is false. For example:

```
x = 2
if x > 3:
  print("x is greater than 3")
else:
  print("x is less than or equal to 3")
```

In this example, if the value of **x** is greater than 3, the first block of code is executed, and if it's less than or equal to 3, the second block of code is executed.

You can also use the **elif** statement to check additional

conditions. For example:

```
x = 5
if x > 10:
    print("x is greater than 10")
elif x > 5:
    print("x is greater than 5 but less than or equal to 10")
else:
    print("x is less than or equal to 5")
```

In this example, the **if** statement checks whether the value of **x** is greater than 10, the **elif** statement checks whether it's greater than 5 but less than or equal to 10, and the **else** statement covers all other cases.

Loops

Loops allow you to repeat a block of code multiple times. Python provides two types of loops: **for** loops and **while** loops.

For Loops

For loops allow you to iterate over a sequence of values, such as a list or a tuple. For example:

```
fruits = ['apple', 'banana', 'cherry']
for fruit in fruits:
    print(fruit)
```

In this example, the **for** loop iterates over the items in the list of **fruits** and prints each item to the console.

You can also use the **range()** function to generate a sequence of numbers to iterate over. For example:

```
for i in range(1, 4):
    print(i)
```

In this example, the **range()** function generates the sequence [**1, 2, 3**], and the **for** loop iterates over each number in the sequence and prints it to the console.

While Loops

While loops allow you to repeat a block of code as long as a certain condition is true. For example:

```
i = 1
while i <= 3:
  print(i)
  i += 1
```

In this example, the **while** loop repeats the block of code as long as the value of **i** is less than or equal to 3.

Conclusion

Python provides a variety of control flow statements to help you write more expressive and efficient programs. By understanding these statements and their syntax, you can write programs that are more flexible and adaptable to different scenarios. Whether you're a beginner or an experienced Python developer, knowing when to use each control flow statement will help you write more readable and maintainable code. With this knowledge, you can make your code more efficient and effective.

Keep in mind that control flow statements should be used appropriately and in a way that makes the most sense for your program. While they can make your code more powerful, using them in the wrong way can also make it harder to understand and maintain.

In conclusion, Python's control flow statements are powerful tools that allow you to create flexible and expressive programs.

With conditional statements and loops, you can control the order in which your code is executed and create more dynamic programs. By understanding these control flow statements and their syntax, you can write more efficient and effective code, no matter what your experience level with Python might be.

I.VIII Python Functions

Functions are a fundamental part of programming in Python. They allow you to break down complex tasks into smaller, more manageable pieces of code, which can be reused throughout your program. In this article, we'll explore the basics of Python functions and how to use them in your programs.

Defining a Function

To define a function in Python, you use the **def** keyword followed by the name of the function, any parameters it takes (if any), and a colon. For example:

```
def greet(name):
  print("Hello, " + name + "!")
```

In this example, we've defined a function called **greet** that takes a single parameter called **name**. When this function is called, it prints the message "Hello, " followed by the value of the **name** parameter and an exclamation point.

Calling a Function

To call a function in Python, you simply use its name followed by any arguments it takes (if any) inside parentheses. For example:

```
greet("Alice")
```

In this example, we're calling the **greet** function with the argument **"Alice"**. When this line of code is executed, the function is called with the value of the **name** set to **"Alice"**, and the message "Hello, Alice!" is printed to the console.

Default Parameters

In Python, you can define default values for parameters in a function. This allows you to call the function without specifying a value for that parameter, and the default value will be used instead. For example:

```python
def greet(name="world"):
    print("Hello, " + name + "!")
```

In this example, we've defined a default value of **"world"** for the **name** parameter. If you call the **greet** function without specifying a value for the **name**, the default value will be used. For example:

```python
greet()
```

In this example, the **greet** function is called without any arguments, so the default value of **"world"** is used, and the message "Hello, world!" is printed on the console.

Returning Values

In Python, functions can also return values, which can be used in other parts of your program. To return a value from a function, you use the **return** keyword followed by the value you want to return. For example:

```python
def add_numbers(x, y):
    return x + y
```

In this example, we've defined a function called **add_numbers** that takes two parameters **x** and **y**. When this function is called, it returns the sum of **x** and **y**. For example:

```python
result = add_numbers(3, 5)
print(result)
```

In this example, the **add_numbers** function is called with the arguments **3** and **5**, and the result of **8** is returned. This result is then stored in the variable **result**, which is printed to the console.

Conclusion

Python functions are a powerful tool that allows you to break down complex tasks into smaller, more manageable pieces of code. By understanding how to define and call functions, use default parameters, and return values, you can create more flexible and dynamic programs. Whether you're a beginner or an experienced Python developer, knowing how to use functions effectively will make your code more efficient and effective.

I.IX Python Import Statement

In Python, the **import** statement is used to import modules into your program. A module is a file that contains Python code and can contain functions, classes, and variables. Importing modules allows you to reuse code from other programs, and can help you write more efficient and effective programs.

Importing a Module

To import a module in Python, you use the **import** statement followed by the name of the module. For example, to import the **math** module, you would use the following code:

```
import math
```

In this example, we're importing the **math** module into our program. Once the module is imported, we can use its functions and variables in our code.

Importing a Function

If you only need to use a single function from a module, you can import just that function instead of the entire module. To import a function from a module, you use the **from** keyword followed by the name of the module, the **import** keyword, and the name of the function. For example, to import the **sqrt** function from the **math** module, you would use the following code:

```
from math import sqrt
```

In this example, we're importing just the **sqrt** function from the **math** module. Once the function is imported, we can use it in our code without needing to reference the module. For example:

```
result = sqrt(16)
```

```
print(result)
```

In this example, the **sqrt** function is called with argument **16**, and the result of **4.0** is printed to the console.

Renaming a Module or Function

If the name of a module or function you want to import conflicts with a name that's already used in your program, you can rename the module or function using the **as** keyword. For example, to import the **math** module with the name **m**, you would use the following code:

```
import math as m
```

In this example, we're importing the **math** module with the name **m**. Once the module is imported, we can use its functions and variables using the **m** prefix. For example:

```
result = m.sqrt(16)
```

```
print(result)
```

In this example, the **sqrt** function from the **math** module is called with argument **16**, and the result of **4.0** is printed to the console.

Importing All Functions and Variables

If you want to import all the functions and variables from a module, you can use the * wildcard character. For example, to import all the functions and variables from the **math** module, you would use the following code:

```
from math import *
```

In this example, we're importing all the functions and variables from the **math** module. Once the module is imported, we can use its functions and variables directly in our code without needing to reference the module. However, it's generally recommended to only import the specific functions and variables that you need, rather than importing everything.

Conclusion

The **import** statement is a powerful tool in Python that allows you to reuse code from other programs and can help you write more efficient and effective programs. By understanding how to import modules and functions, and how to rename them to avoid naming conflicts, you can create more flexible and dynamic programs. Whether you're a beginner or an experienced Python developer, knowing how to use the **import** statement effectively will make your code more efficient and effective.

I.X Anaconda Spyder

What is Anaconda Spyder?

Anaconda Spyder is an integrated development environment (IDE) designed for data science and scientific computing using the Python programming language. It's part of the Anaconda distribution, which is a package manager and environment manager for Python.

Spyder provides a user-friendly interface for developing and debugging Python code and includes a variety of tools and features that are useful for data analysis, visualization, and modeling. Some of these features include:

- An interactive console that allows you to execute Python code and view the output in real-time
- A variable explorer that lets you view and modify the values of variables in your code
- A code editor with syntax highlighting, code folding, and autocomplete functionality
- A debugger that allows you to step through your code and debug errors
- Built-in support for popular Python libraries such as NumPy, pandas, and matplotlib

Installing Anaconda Spyder

To install Anaconda Spyder, you first need to download and install the Anaconda distribution. You can download Anaconda from the official website (https://www.anaconda.com/products/individual), which provides installers for Windows, macOS, and Linux.

Once you've downloaded and installed Anaconda, you can open

Spyder by launching the Anaconda Navigator application, which provides a graphical user interface for managing your Anaconda environments and launching applications such as Spyder.

Using Anaconda Spyder

When you first open Spyder, you'll see a layout that consists of several panels, including a code editor, console, and variable explorer. You can use these panels to write and execute Python code, and to view the output and results of your code.

To create a new Python script in Spyder, you can click on the "File" menu and select "New File". This will open a new tab in the code editor where you can start writing your code.

To execute Python code in Spyder, you can either type the code directly into the console or the code editor and press "Enter", or you can run the entire script by clicking on the "Run" button in the toolbar or by pressing "F5". The output of your code will be displayed in the console.

You can also use the variable explorer to view and modify the values of variables in your code. To view a variable in the variable explorer, simply click on its name in the code editor or console. To modify a variable, you can double-click on its value in the variable explorer and enter a new value.

Conclusion

Anaconda Spyder is a powerful and user-friendly IDE for data science and scientific computing using the Python programming language. With its interactive console, variable explorer, code editor, and debugger, Spyder provides a comprehensive set of tools and features that are essential for data analysis and modeling. Whether you're a beginner or an experienced data scientist, Spyder is a great choice for developing and debugging Python code in a data-rich environment.

I.XI Scripting in Python

What is Scripting?

Scripting is a type of programming that involves writing scripts, which are sequences of instructions that are executed by a computer. Scripts are typically used to automate repetitive tasks or to perform complex operations that would be difficult or time-consuming to do manually.

Scripting languages are programming languages that are specifically designed for writing scripts. These languages are typically easy to learn and use, and they often have built-in functions and libraries that are useful for common scripting tasks.

Python is a popular programming language that is widely used for scripting, as well as for web development, scientific computing, and other applications.

Why use Python for Scripting?

Python is a great choice for scripting for several reasons:

- Easy to learn: Python has a simple and intuitive syntax that makes it easy to learn and use. This makes it a great choice for beginners who want to get started with scripting.

- Large community and ecosystem: Python has a large and active community of developers who have created many useful libraries and tools for Python. This means that you can often find pre-existing code or modules to use for your scripting tasks.

- Cross-platform: Python is a cross-platform language, which means that scripts written in Python can run on any operating system, including Windows, macOS, and Linux.

- High-level: Python is a high-level language, which means that it abstracts away many of the low-level details of programming, such as memory management and pointer arithmetic. This makes it easier to write and read code, and it also reduces the likelihood of bugs and errors.

Getting Started with Python Scripting

To get started with Python scripting, you first need to have Python installed on your computer. You can download Python from the official website (https://www.python.org/downloads/), which provides installers for Windows, macOS, and Linux.

Once you have Python installed, you can start writing scripts using a text editor or an integrated development environment (IDE) such as PyCharm or Visual Studio Code.

To write a simple Python script, create a new text file with a .py extension and add the following code:

```
print("Hello, World!")
```

Save the file and then open a terminal or command prompt and navigate to the directory where the file is saved. Type the following command to run the script:

```
$ python script.py
```

This will execute the script and print "Hello, World!" to the console.

Conclusion

Python is a great language for scripting, thanks to its simplicity, large community, cross-platform support, and high-level features. Whether you're a beginner or an experienced programmer, Python can help you automate tasks, build tools, and create powerful scripts that can save you time and effort. So why not give Python scripting a try and see what you can accomplish!

I.XII Python Tips and Tricks

Python is a powerful programming language that offers a lot of flexibility and ease of use. Whether you're a beginner or an experienced programmer, there are always new tips and tricks to learn that can help you improve your coding skills and write more efficient and effective code.

In this section, we'll explore some of the most useful Python tips and tricks that can help you become a better Python developer.

Tip 1: List Comprehensions

List comprehensions are a concise and powerful way to create lists in Python. They allow you to create a list in a single line of code by applying a function or expression to each item in an existing list.

For example, suppose you have a list of numbers and you want to create a new list that contains only the even numbers. You could use a for loop to iterate over the list and append each even number to a new list:

```
numbers = [1, 2, 3, 4, 5, 6, 7, 8, 9]
even_numbers = []
for n in numbers:
    if n % 2 == 0:
        even_numbers.append(n)
```

With a list comprehension, you can achieve the same result in a single line of code:

```
numbers = [1, 2, 3, 4, 5, 6, 7, 8, 9]
even_numbers = [n for n in numbers if n % 2 == 0]
```

This code creates a new list called **even_numbers** that contains only the even numbers from the original **numbers** list.

Tip 2: Default Arguments in Functions

Python allows you to specify default values for function arguments. This can be useful when you want to provide a default value for an argument, but still, allow the user to override that value if necessary.

For example, suppose you have a function that takes two arguments: **x** and **y**. You want to provide a default value of 0 for **y**, but still allow the user to specify a different value if they want to:

```
def my_function(x, y=0):
  return x + y
```

With this code, you can call **my_function** with just one argument, and the default value of 0 will be used for **y**:

```
result = my_function(5)
print(result) # Output: 5
```

You can also override the default value by providing a value for **y**:

```
result = my_function(5, 10)
print(result) # Output: 15
```

Tip 3: Using Enumerate

The **enumerate** function is a handy tool for iterating over a list and keeping track of the index of each item. It returns an iterator that yields tuples containing the index and value of each item in the list.

For example, suppose you have a list of names and you want to print out each name along with its index:

```
names = ['Alice', 'Bob', 'Charlie']
```

```
for i, name in enumerate(names):
    print(i, name)
```

This code will output:

```
0 Alice
1 Bob
2 Charlie
```

Tip 4: Using Zip

The **zip** function is another useful tool for working with lists. It takes two or more lists as arguments and returns an iterator that yields tuples containing the corresponding elements from each list.

For example, suppose you have two lists of numbers, and you want to create a new list that contains the sum of the corresponding numbers in each list:

```
a = [1, 2, 3]
b =[4, 5, 6]
result = []
for i in range(len(a)):
    result.append(a[i] + b[i])
    print(result)
```

This code will output:

```
[5, 7, 9]
```

With the `zip` function, you can achieve the same result more concisely:

```
a = [1, 2, 3]
b = [4, 5, 6]
result = [x + y for x, y in zip(a, b)]
```

```
print(result)
```

This code also outputs:

```
[5, 7, 9]
```

Tip 5: Context Managers

Context managers are a way to manage resources like files or network connections safely and conveniently. They allow you to automatically open and close resources without having to worry about errors or exceptions. For example, suppose you have a file that you want to read from, and you want to make sure that the file is properly closed when you're done reading from it:

```
with open('myfile.txt', 'r') as f:
    data = f.read()
    # Do something with the data
```

The `with` statement creates a context in which the file is open for reading. When the code inside the `with` block is finished executing, the file is automatically closed, even if an error occurs.

Conclusion

These are just a few of the many tips and tricks that can help you become a more efficient and effective Python developer. By mastering these techniques, you can write cleaner, more concise code that is easier to read and maintain.

Tip 6: Using List Comprehensions

List comprehensions are a powerful way to create lists in Python. They allow you to create a new list by iterating over an existing iterable and applying a function to each element. List comprehensions are often more concise and easier to read than using a for loop and appending to a list.

For example, suppose you have a list of numbers and you want to create a new list that contains only the even numbers:

```
numbers = [1, 2, 3, 4, 5, 6, 7, 8, 9, 10]
evens = [x for x in numbers if x % 2 == 0]
print(evens)
```

This code will output:

```
[2, 4, 6, 8, 10]
```

Tip 7: Using the Else Clause in Loops

The **else** clause in a loop is executed when the loop finishes normally, without being interrupted by a **break** statement. This can be useful when you want to perform some final action after a loop has been completed.

For example, suppose you want to check if a number is a prime by testing if it is divisible by any number between 2 and the number itself. If the number is not divisible by any of these numbers, then it is prime. You can use the **else** clause in a **for** loop to handle the case when the number is prime:

```
num = 17
for i in range(2, num):
    if num % i == 0:
        print(num, 'is not prime')
        break
else:
    print(num, 'is prime')
```

This code will output:

```
17 is prime
```

Conclusion

Python is a powerful language with many features and tricks that can help you write more efficient and effective code. By mastering these techniques, you can become a more productive developer and create better Python applications.

I.XIII What to Do and What Not to Do in Python

Python is a powerful language with many features and capabilities. It can be easy to get carried away with all the things you can do in Python, but it's important to keep in mind that there are some best practices to follow and some things to avoid. In this section, we'll discuss what to do and what not to do in Python.

What to Do

1. Write Clear and Readable Code

One of the most important things to do in Python is to write clear and readable code. This means using meaningful variable names, writing comments to explain your code, and breaking up long blocks of code into smaller, more manageable pieces.

2. Use Built-in Functions and Libraries

Python has a large standard library and many built-in functions that can save you time and effort when writing code. Take advantage of these built-in functions and libraries whenever possible, as they are often optimized for performance and reliability.

3. Use List Comprehensions

List comprehensions are a powerful way to create lists in Python. They allow you to create a new list by iterating over an existing iterable and applying a function to each element. List comprehensions are often more concise and easier to read than using a for loop and appending to a list.

4. Use Exceptions for Error Handling

Python has a powerful exception-handling mechanism that

allows you to handle errors and exceptions gracefully. When writing code, make sure to use exceptions for error handling, as this can make your code more reliable and easier to maintain.

5. Use Context Managers

Context managers are a way to manage resources like files or network connections safely and conveniently. They allow you to automatically open and close resources without having to worry about errors or exceptions. Use context managers whenever possible, as they can help prevent resource leaks and make your code more reliable.

What Not to Do

1. Use Global Variables

Global variables are variables that are defined outside of a function or class. While global variables can be useful in some cases, they should generally be avoided, as they can make your code harder to understand and maintain. Instead, use local variables within functions and classes, as this can make your code more modular and easier to test.

2. Use Mutable Objects as Default Arguments

When defining a function in Python, you can specify default arguments that are used if the function is called without providing a value for that argument. However, if you use a mutable object as a default argument, you can run into unexpected behavior, as the same object is reused across multiple function calls. To avoid this, use immutable objects like None or integers as default arguments, or create a new object within the function.

3. Use Multiple Inheritance

Multiple inheritance is the ability to inherit from multiple base classes in Python. While this can be a powerful feature, it can also lead to complex and hard-to-understand code. When possible, use single inheritance or composition to achieve the same result.

4. Use Unnecessary Type Conversions

Python is a dynamically typed language, which means that you don't need to specify the data type of a variable when you declare it. However, if you use type conversions unnecessarily, you can introduce performance issues or bugs. Only use type conversions when necessary, and make sure to test your code thoroughly.

5. Ignore Exceptions

When an exception is raised in Python, it's important to handle it gracefully. Ignoring exceptions can lead to unexpected behavior or crashes, and can make your code harder to debug. Always make sure to handle exceptions in your code, even if it's just by logging an error message.

Conclusion

Python is a powerful language with many features and capabilities. By following these best practices and avoiding common pitfalls, you can write more reliable and maintainable Python code. Remember to write clear and readable code, use built-in functions and libraries, and take advantage of powerful language features like list comprehensions and context managers. And be sure to avoid common mistakes like using global variables, mutable objects as default arguments, and unnecessary type conversions. With these tips in mind, you'll be well on your way to writing high-quality Python code that is both efficient and effective.

I.XIV Hands-on Creating a
Python Calculator

In this section, we will be creating a simple calculator using Python. This calculator will be able to perform basic arithmetic operations such as addition, subtraction, multiplication, and division. We will be using Python's built-in functions and data types to create this calculator.

Step 1: Define the Problem
Before we start writing code, let's define the problem we want to solve. In this case, we want to create a calculator that can perform simple arithmetic calculations such as addition, subtraction, multiplication, and division.

Step 2: Plan the Solution
Now that we have defined the problem, let's plan how to solve it. We need to create a program that asks the user for two numbers and an operator, performs the corresponding calculation, and displays the result. Here are the steps we need to follow:

1. Ask the user to input the first number

2. Ask the user to input the second number

3. Ask the user to input the operator (+, -, *, /)

4. Perform the calculation based on the operator

5. Display the result

Step 3: Write the Code
Now that we have a plan, let's write the code. Here's the code to create a simple calculator in Python:

```
# Ask the user to input the first number
```

```python
num1 = float(input("Enter first number: "))

# Ask the user to input the second number
num2 = float(input("Enter second number: "))

# Ask the user to input the operator (+, -, *, /)
operator = input("Enter operator (+, -, *, /): ")

# Perform the calculation based on the operator
if operator == '+':
    result = num1 + num2
elif operator == '-':
    result = num1 - num2
elif operator == '*':
    result = num1 * num2
elif operator == '/':
    result = num1 / num2
else:
    print("Invalid operator")

# Display the result
print("Result:", result)
```

Let's break down this code. First, we ask the user to input the first number using the **input()** function. We convert the input to a float using the **float()** function and store it in the variable **num1**.

Next, we ask the user to input the second number using the same process and store it in the variable **num2**.

Then, we ask the user to input the operator using the **input()**

function and store it in the variable **operator**.

After that, we use an **if** statement to perform the calculation based on the operator. If the operator is +, we add the two numbers and store the result in the variable **result**. If the operator is -, we subtract the second number from the first number and store the result in **result**. Similarly, we perform multiplication and division based on the operator. If the operator is none of the above, we print "Invalid operator".

Finally, we display the result using the **print()** function and concatenating the string "Result:" with the value of the **result** variable.

Step 4: Test the Calculator

Now that we have written the code, let's test the calculator. Run the program and enter two numbers and an operator when prompted. Here are some sample inputs and outputs:

Test 1

Enter first number: 5

Enter second number: 2

Enter operator (+, -, *, /): +

Result: 7.0

Test 2

Enter first number: 10

Enter second number: 3

Enter operator (+, -, *, /): /

Result: 3.3333333333333335

Test 3

Enter first number: 8

Enter second number: 4

Enter operator (+, -, *, /): %

Invalid operator

Step 5: Enhance the Calculator
Congratulations! You have created a simple calculator using Python. However, there are some improvements you can make to this program to make it more user-friendly and robust. Here are some suggestions:

- Add input validation to ensure that the user enters valid numbers and operators.

- Allow the user to perform multiple calculations in the same session without having to restart the program.

- Add more functionality, such as calculating square roots, exponents, and trigonometric functions.

- Create a graphical user interface (GUI) using a library such as Tkinter or PyQt.

With these enhancements, you can create a more powerful and versatile calculator using Python.

Conclusion

In this section, we have learned how to create a basic calculator using Python. We started by defining the variables and prompting the user to enter the inputs. Then, we used conditional statements to perform the calculation based on the operator. Finally, we displayed the result to the user.

Creating a calculator is a good exercise for beginners to get familiar with basic programming concepts such as variables, data types, operators, and conditional statements. It is also a useful tool for performing calculations in your daily life or work.

Python provides a powerful and easy-to-use programming language that is ideal for creating calculators and other simple applications. With its rich library of modules and tools, Python has become a popular choice for data analysis, machine learning, and web development.

We hope that this section has provided you with a good foundation for creating your own Python calculator. Happy coding!

I.XV Overview of the most commonly used Python libraries for data science and machine

Python is a popular programming language for data science and machine learning due to its versatility, ease of use, and a large collection of libraries and tools. In this article, we will provide an overview of some of the most commonly used Python libraries for data science and machine learning.

1. NumPy

NumPy is a library for numerical computing in Python. It provides powerful data structures for working with arrays and matrices, as well as a large collection of mathematical functions for operations such as linear algebra, Fourier analysis, and random number generation. NumPy is a fundamental library for data science and machine learning in Python.

2. Pandas

Pandas is a library for data manipulation and analysis in Python. It provides data structures for working with labeled data such as tables, time series, and matrices. Pandas provides tools for data cleaning, merging, reshaping, and aggregation. It is widely used in data science and machine learning applications for data preprocessing and exploratory data analysis.

3. Matplotlib

Matplotlib is a library for data visualization in Python. It provides a variety of charts and graphs for exploring and presenting data, including line plots, scatter plots, histograms, and bar charts. Matplotlib is highly customizable and can be used to create publication-quality plots for scientific and engineering applications.

4. Seaborn

Seaborn is a library for statistical data visualization in Python. It provides a high-level interface for creating attractive and informative statistical graphics, such as heatmaps, pair plots, and violin plots. Seaborn is built on top of Matplotlib and integrates well with Pandas data structures.

5. Scikit-learn

Scikit-learn is a library for machine learning in Python. It provides a variety of algorithms for classification, regression, clustering, and dimensionality reduction. Scikit-learn is designed for ease of use and provides a consistent API for fitting, evaluating, and tuning machine learning models. It is widely used in data science and machine learning applications.

6. TensorFlow

TensorFlow is a library for machine learning and deep learning in Python. It provides a flexible and scalable platform for building and training machine learning models, including neural networks. TensorFlow is widely used in applications such as image and speech recognition, natural language processing, and robotics.

7. Keras

Keras is a high-level neural networks library written in Python. It provides a simple and intuitive interface for building and training deep learning models, including convolutional neural networks (CNNs), recurrent neural networks (RNNs), and generative adversarial networks (GANs). Keras can be used with TensorFlow or other backend engines.

8. PyTorch

PyTorch is a library for machine learning and deep learning in Python. It provides a dynamic and flexible platform for building and training machine learning models, including neural networks. PyTorch emphasizes ease of use and provides a fast and efficient implementation of automatic differentiation, a key technique for training deep learning models.

Conclusion

Python provides a rich ecosystem of libraries and tools for data science and machine learning. In this article, we have provided an overview of some of the most commonly used libraries, including NumPy, Pandas, Matplotlib, Seaborn, Scikit-learn, TensorFlow, Keras, and PyTorch. These libraries provide powerful and flexible tools for data analysis, visualization, and modeling, making Python a popular choice for data science and machine learning applications.

I.XVI learning, including NumPy, Pandas, Matplotlib, and Scikit-learn

Python is a popular programming language among data scientists and machine learning professionals. One of the reasons for this popularity is the vast array of libraries and tools available for these fields. In this section, we will introduce four of the most commonly used Python libraries in data science and machine learning: NumPy, Pandas, Matplotlib, and Scikit-learn.

1. NumPy

NumPy (Numerical Python) is a fundamental library for numerical computing in Python. It provides support for large, multi-dimensional arrays and matrices, along with a wide range of mathematical functions to operate on these arrays.

Key Features:

- Efficient array operations
- Broadcasting for element-wise array operations
- Mathematical functions
- Linear algebra, Fourier analysis, and random number capabilities

An example of including Numpy in a Python script:

```
import numpy as np
# Create a 2D Numpy array
arr = np.array([[1, 2, 3], [4, 5, 6]])
# Print the array
print(arr)
```

In this example, we import the Numpy library using the import statement and alias it as np for brevity. Then we create a 2D Numpy array using the np.array() method, and finally, we print the array using the print() function.

2. Pandas

Pandas is a powerful library for data manipulation and analysis in Python. It introduces two essential data structures, Series and DataFrame, designed to make it easy to work with structured data.

Key Features:

- Data import/export from various formats (CSV, Excel, JSON, etc.)
- Data cleaning and transformation
- Handling missing data
- Merging, joining, and concatenating datasets
- Grouping and aggregation
- Time series analysis

An example of how to include Pandas in a Python script:

```python
import pandas as pd
# Load data from a CSV file
data = pd.read_csv('my_data.csv')
# Print the first 10 rows of the data
print(data.head(10))
# Get some basic statistics about the data
print(data.describe())
# Filter the data to only include rows where the 'age' column is greater than or equal to 30
filtered_data = data[data['age'] >= 30]
# Write the filtered data to a new CSV file
filtered_data.to_csv('filtered_data.csv', index=False)
```

In this example, we start by importing Pandas using the import statement. We then load some data from a CSV file using the read_csv() function, which returns a Pandas DataFrame object. We can then use various DataFrame methods to manipulate the data, such as head() to print the first few rows of the data, describe() to get some basic statistics about the data, and filtering the data using boolean indexing. Finally, we can write the filtered data back to a CSV file using the to_csv() method.

3. Matplotlib

Matplotlib is a powerful plotting library for Python that enables users to create high-quality static, animated, and interactive visualizations. It provides a MATLAB-like interface, with numerous customization options.

Key Features:

- Line plots, scatter plots, bar plots, and histograms
- Heatmaps, contour plots, and 3D plots
- Customization of plot appearance (colors, markers, labels, etc.)
- Interactive plots and animations

An example of including Matplotlib in a Python script to create a simple line plot:

```python
import matplotlib.pyplot as plt
# create some data
x = [1, 2, 3, 4, 5]
y = [2, 4, 6, 8, 10]
# create a line plot
plt.plot(x, y)
# add labels and a title
plt.xlabel('X-axis')
plt.ylabel('Y-axis')
plt.title('Line Plot')
# display the plot
```

```
plt.show()
```

In this example, we first import the pyplot module from Matplotlib using the import statement and give it an alias plt to make it easier to use. We then create some sample data for the x and y variables.

Next, we use the plot() function to create a line plot using the data we just created. We then use the xlabel(), ylabel(), and title() functions to add labels and a title to the plot.

Finally, we use the show() function to display the plot in a new window. This will open a window with the plot displayed inside it.

4. Scikit-learn

Scikit-learn is a popular machine learning library in Python, built on top of NumPy, SciPy, and Matplotlib. It provides a wide range of algorithms and tools for classification, regression, clustering, dimensionality reduction, model selection, and preprocessing.

Key Features:

- Simple and efficient tools for data mining and data analysis
- Accessible to both experts and non-experts in machine learning
- Extensive documentation and examples
- Open source, commercially usable

An example of including Scikit-learn in a Python script:

```
import pandas as pd
from sklearn.linear_model import LinearRegression
# Load data from a CSV file
data = pd.read_csv('data.csv')
# Split the data into features and target variable
```

```
X = data.drop('target', axis=1)
y = data['target']
# Train a linear regression model on the data
model = LinearRegression()
model.fit(X, y)
# Make predictions on new data
new_data = pd.DataFrame([[1, 2, 3], [4, 5, 6]],
columns=['feature1', 'feature2', 'feature3'])
predictions = model.predict(new_data)
# Print the predictions
print(predictions)
```

In this example, we first import pandas to load and manipulate the data, and then import the LinearRegression class from sklearn.linear_model to train a linear regression model on the data. We then split the data into features and target variable, and fit the model on the features and target. Finally, we make predictions on new data using the trained model, and print the predictions.

Conclusion

In this section, we have provided an overview of the four most commonly used Python libraries in data science and machine learning: NumPy, Pandas, Matplotlib, and Scikit-learn. These libraries provide essential tools for working with data, performing mathematical operations, visualizing data, and building predictive models. With these libraries, you can perform complex data analyses and develop powerful machine-learning models, making Python an indispensable tool in the field of data science and machine learning.

II. DATA PREPARATION WITH NUMPY AND PANDAS

Data preparation is a critical step in the data science process, and NumPy and Pandas are two of the most popular libraries used for this task in Python. NumPy provides support for large, multi-dimensional arrays and matrices, while Pandas provides tools for data manipulation and analysis. In this chapter, we will explore the key features of NumPy and Pandas and learn how to use these libraries to prepare and manipulate data for further analysis. We will cover topics such as importing data into NumPy and Pandas, data cleaning and preprocessing, data exploration and visualization, and more. By the end of this chapter, you will have a solid understanding of how to use NumPy and Pandas to prepare your data for analysis in Python.

II.I Introduction to NumPy and Pandas libraries

Data is the backbone of any data science project, and data manipulation is a critical step in the data science process. NumPy and Pandas are two of the most popular Python libraries used for data manipulation and analysis.

NumPy (Numerical Python) is a Python library that provides support for large, multi-dimensional arrays and matrices, along with a large collection of mathematical functions to operate on these arrays. It is a fundamental library for scientific computing in Python and is often used in conjunction with other data science libraries such as Pandas, Matplotlib, and Scikit-learn.

Pandas, on the other hand, is a library built on top of NumPy that provides tools for data manipulation and analysis. It offers data structures for efficiently storing and manipulating large, complex datasets, including support for handling missing or incomplete data, time series data, and relational databases.

In this section, we will provide an introduction to NumPy and Pandas and cover some of their key features and functionalities.

NumPy

NumPy is an open-source numerical computing library for Python that provides support for large, multi-dimensional arrays and matrices. It is built on top of the C programming language, which makes it fast and efficient, and provides a large collection of mathematical functions that can be applied to these arrays.

One of the key advantages of NumPy is its ability to handle large datasets efficiently. NumPy arrays are much more efficient than Python lists for handling large amounts of data, as they are stored in contiguous blocks of memory and can be accessed and manipulated much faster than lists.

In addition to its efficient handling of large datasets, NumPy provides a wide range of mathematical functions that can be applied to these arrays, including basic arithmetic operations, statistical functions, and linear algebra operations. NumPy also provides support for random number generation and Fourier transforms, making it a comprehensive library for scientific computing in Python.

Pandas

Pandas is a library built on top of NumPy that provides tools for data manipulation and analysis. It is particularly useful for handling large, complex datasets, and provides data structures for efficiently storing and manipulating this data.

The two primary data structures provided by Pandas are Series and DataFrame. A Series is a one-dimensional array-like object that can hold any data type, while a DataFrame is a two-dimensional table-like data structure that can hold multiple Series objects.

Pandas provides a wide range of tools for data manipulation and analysis, including support for filtering, sorting, grouping, and aggregating data, as well as handling missing or incomplete data, time series data, and relational databases. It also provides powerful data visualization tools for exploring and visualizing datasets.

Conclusion

NumPy and Pandas are two of the most widely used Python libraries for data manipulation and analysis. NumPy provides support for large, multi-dimensional arrays and matrices, along with a large collection of mathematical functions, while Pandas provides tools for data manipulation and analysis, including support for handling large, complex datasets and powerful data visualization tools.

In the next section, we will dive deeper into the key features of NumPy and Pandas and explore some practical examples of how to use these libraries for data manipulation and analysis in Python.

II.II Reading and manipulating
data with Pandas

Pandas is a popular Python library for data analysis and manipulation. Pandas is a Python library used for data manipulation and analysis. It is built on top of the NumPy library and provides data structures like Series and DataFrame, which make data manipulation easy and intuitive. Pandas can handle a wide range of data sources, including CSV, Excel, SQL databases, and more. In this section, we'll explore the basics of reading and manipulating data with Pandas.

Reading data with Pandas

Pandas provides a variety of methods for reading data from different sources. The most commonly used method is the read_csv() function, which reads data from a CSV file and returns a DataFrame object. Here's an example:

```
import pandas as pd

df = pd.read_csv('data.csv')
```

This code reads the data from a CSV file named data.csv and stores it in a DataFrame object named data. The read_csv() function has many options for customizing the reading process, such as specifying column names, handling missing values, and setting the data types of columns. You can inspect the shape, columns, index, and summary statistics of a DataFrame using the following methods:

```
df.shape # returns the number of rows and columns
df.columns # returns the column names
df.index # returns the row labels
df.describe() # returns descriptive statistics
```

You can also view the first or last few rows of a DataFrame using the head or tail methods:

```
df.head() # returns the first 5 rows by default
df.tail(10) # returns the last 10 rows
```

Manipulating data with Pandas

Pandas offers many ways to manipulate data in a DataFrame, such as selecting, filtering, sorting, grouping, aggregating, merging, reshaping, and more. Here are some examples of common data manipulation tasks:

- **Selecting columns or rows:** You can use the [] operator or the loc or iloc methods to select columns or rows by name or position. For example:

```
df["name"] # returns the column "name" as a Series
df[["name", "age"]] # returns a subset of columns as a DataFrame
df.loc[0] # returns the first row as a Series
df.loc[0:5] # returns a slice of rows as a DataFrame
df.iloc[0] # returns the first row as a Series by position
df.iloc[0:5] # returns a slice of rows as a DataFrame by position
```

- **Filtering rows:** You can use boolean expressions to filter rows based on some conditions. For example:

```
df[df["age"] > 30] # returns only the rows where age is greater than 30
df[(df["age"] > 30) & (df["gender"] == "F")] # returns only the rows where age is greater than 30 and gender is F
```

- **Sorting rows or columns:** You can use the sort_values or sort_index methods to sort a DataFrame by values or labels. For example:

```
df.sort_values(by="age") # returns a DataFrame sorted by age in ascending order
df.sort_values(by="age", ascending=False) # returns a DataFrame sorted by age in descending order
df.sort_index() # returns a DataFrame sorted by row labels
```

- Grouping and aggregating: You can use the groupby method to group a DataFrame by one or more columns and apply some aggregation functions to each group. For example:

```
df.groupby("gender")["age"].mean() # returns the average age for each gender
df.groupby(["gender", "city"])["salary"].sum() # returns the total salary for each gender-city combination
```

- Merging and joining: You can use the merge or join methods to combine two DataFrames based on some common columns or indexes. For example:

```
df1 = pd.read_csv("data1.csv")
df2 = pd.read_csv("data2.csv")
pd.merge(df1, df2, on="id") # returns a DataFrame with columns from both df1 and df2 based on id
pd.join(df1, df2, on="id") # same as above but using join method
```

- Reshaping and pivoting: You can use the reshape or pivot methods to change the layout of a DataFrame. For example:

```
df.pivot(index="name", columns="city", values="salary") # returns a DataFrame with name as rows, city as columns, and salary as values
```

Conclusion

In this section, we've explored the basics of reading and manipulating data with Pandas. We've seen how to read data from various sources, and how to perform common manipulations like selecting, filtering, and aggregating data. Pandas is a powerful tool for data manipulation and analysis and is widely used in the data science community. With these basic skills, you'll be well on your way to working with large datasets and extracting valuable insights from them.

II.III Cleaning and preprocessing data

Data cleaning and preprocessing are essential steps in any data analysis or machine learning project. Pandas provides powerful tools to clean and preprocess data, allowing us to handle missing values, remove duplicates, transform data, and more.

Handling Missing Values

Missing values are a common issue in real-world datasets. They can be caused by various factors, such as data collection errors or incomplete data. Pandas provides several methods to handle missing values:

- **isnull()**: returns a DataFrame of boolean values indicating which values are missing or NaN.

- **notnull()**: returns the opposite of **isnull()**.

- **dropna()**: removes any row that contains at least one NaN value.

- **fillna()**: fills in missing values with a specified value or method, such as the mean or median.

Checking for Missing Values

Before handling missing values, we need to check if there are any missing values in the dataset. We can use the **isna()** method to check for missing values in a Pandas DataFrame:

```
import pandas as pd
# load the dataset
df = pd.read_csv('data.csv')
# check for missing values
print(df.isna().sum())
```

The **isna()** method returns a DataFrame of the same shape as the original DataFrame, where each element is a Boolean value indicating whether the corresponding element is missing or not. We can use the **sum()** method to count the number of missing values in each column.

Dropping Missing Values

One way to handle missing values is to simply remove the rows or columns that contain them. We can use the **dropna()** method to drop rows or columns that contain missing values:

```
# drop rows with missing values
df = df.dropna()
# drop columns with missing values
df = df.dropna(axis=1)
```

The **dropna()** method returns a new DataFrame with the missing values removed. By default, it drops rows that contain any missing values. We can set the **axis** parameter to 1 to drop columns instead.

Filling Missing Values

Another way to handle missing values is to fill them with some value. We can use the **fillna()** method to fill missing values with a specified value:

```
# fill missing values with 0
df = df.fillna(0)
# fill missing values with the mean of each column
df = df.fillna(df.mean())
```

The **fillna()** method returns a new DataFrame with the missing values filled. We can pass a scalar value to fill all missing values with the same value, or a dictionary of column names and values to fill each column with a different value.

Removing Duplicates

Duplicates are another common issue in datasets. They can be caused by data collection errors or data storage issues. Pandas provides the **drop_duplicates()** method to remove duplicate rows from a DataFrame:

```
# drop duplicate rows
df = df.drop_duplicates()
```

The **drop_duplicates()** method returns a new DataFrame with the duplicate rows removed. By default, it considers all columns when identifying duplicates. We can pass a list of column names to the **subset** parameter to consider only the specified columns.

Transforming Data

Data transformation is the process of converting data from one format to another or changing the structure of the data. Pandas provides various methods to transform data.

Applying Functions

We can apply a function to each element or row of a DataFrame using the **apply()** method:

```
# apply a function to each element
df = df.apply(lambda x: x * 2)
# apply a function to each row
df = df.apply(lambda row: row['col1'] + row['col2'], axis=1)
```

The **apply()** method applies the specified function to each element or row of the DataFrame and returns a new DataFrame.

Mapping Values

When working with data, it's common to need to map values from one set to another. For example, you may have a dataset that includes country codes and you want to map them to country names. Pandas provide several ways to perform these kinds of mappings.

Using map()

One way to map values in a Pandas DataFrame or Series is to use the **map()** method. This method takes a dictionary or function and applies it to the values in the DataFrame or Series.

Let's start with a simple example. Suppose we have a DataFrame with a column of colors represented as strings:

```
import pandas as pd
data = {
    'color': ['red', 'green', 'blue', 'red', 'green']
}
df = pd.DataFrame(data)
```

We can create a dictionary that maps the colors to hex codes:

```
color_map = {
    'red': '#FF0000',
    'green': '#00FF00',
    'blue': '#0000FF'
}
```

And then apply this map using **map()**:

```
df['color_hex'] = df['color'].map(color_map)
```

The resulting DataFrame will have a new column, **'color_hex'**, with the corresponding hex codes.

Using replace()

Another way to map values in a Pandas DataFrame or Series is to use the **replace()** method. This method takes a dictionary or list of tuples and applies it to the values in the DataFrame or Series.

For example, suppose we have a DataFrame with a column of country codes:

```
data = {
  'country_code': ['US', 'CA', 'MX', 'US', 'MX']
}
df = pd.DataFrame(data)
```

We can create a dictionary that maps the country codes to country names:

```
country_map = {
  'US': 'United States',
  'CA': 'Canada',
  'MX': 'Mexico'
}
```

And then apply this map using **replace()**:

```
df['country'] = df['country_code'].replace(country_map)
```

The resulting DataFrame will have a new column, **'country'**, with the corresponding country names.

Using apply()

A more general way to map values in a Pandas DataFrame or Series is to use the **apply()** method with a function. This method applies the function to each value in the DataFrame or Series.

For example, suppose we have a DataFrame with a column of ages:

```
data = {
```

```
  'age': [25, 30, 40, 22, 35]
}
df = pd.DataFrame(data)
```

We can create a function that maps ages to age groups:

```
def age_group(age):
  if age < 30:
    return 'young'
  elif age < 40:
    return 'middle-aged'
  else:
    return 'old'
df['age_group'] = df['age'].apply(age_group)
```

The resulting DataFrame will have a new column, **'age_group'**, with the corresponding age group for each age.

Conclusion

Mapping values is a common operation when working with data. In this section, we explored three ways to map values in a Pandas DataFrame or Series: using **map()**, using **replace()**, and using **apply()** with a function. Depending on your use case, one of these methods may be more appropriate than the others.

Handling categorical data

Handling categorical data with Pandas is a common task in data preprocessing for machine learning applications.

What is Categorical Data?

Categorical data is data that can be divided into categories or groups. For example, gender, color, or size can be classified into different categories. Categorical data can be further divided into nominal and ordinal categories.

- Nominal data: Nominal data represents categories that cannot be ordered or ranked. Examples of nominal data include color, nationality, and type of animal.

- Ordinal data: Ordinal data represents categories that can be ranked or ordered. Examples of ordinal data include education level, income range, and survey responses.

Encoding Categorical Data

Machine learning algorithms require numerical inputs, and categorical data needs to be encoded to be used in these models. Pandas provides several ways to encode categorical data.

Label Encoding

Label encoding is the process of converting each categorical value into a numerical value. The **LabelEncoder** class in the **sklearn.preprocessing** module can be used for this task.

```
from sklearn.preprocessing import LabelEncoder
le = LabelEncoder()
df['Gender_encoded'] = le.fit_transform(df['Gender'])
```

This code creates a new column called 'Gender_encoded' and populates it with the numerical encoding of the 'Gender' column. The **fit_transform()** method is used to fit the label encoder to the 'Gender' column and transform it into numerical values.

One-Hot Encoding

One-hot encoding is the process of converting each categorical value into a binary vector. The **get_dummies()** function in Pandas can be used to perform one-hot encoding.

```
gender_dummies       =       pd.get_dummies(df['Gender'],
prefix='Gender')
df = pd.concat([df, gender_dummies], axis=1)
```

This code creates new binary columns for each unique value in the 'Gender' column. The **prefix** parameter is used to specify a prefix for the new column names.

Binary Encoding

Binary encoding is the process of converting each unique categorical value into a binary code. The **category_encoders** library provides a **BinaryEncoder** class for this task.

```
import category_encoders as ce
encoder = ce.BinaryEncoder(cols=['Gender'])
df = encoder.fit_transform(df)
```

This code creates new binary columns for each unique value in the 'Gender' column and combines them to create a single binary code for each value.

Conclusion

Handling categorical data is an important step in data preprocessing for machine learning applications. Pandas provides several methods to encode categorical data, including label encoding, one-hot encoding, and binary encoding. The choice of encoding method depends on the specific requirements of the machine learning model being used.

DataScaling and normalization

Data scaling and normalization are essential techniques in

data preparation for machine learning. The purpose of these techniques is to transform numerical data into a standardized range to facilitate machine learning algorithms' better performance. In this section, we will explore how to use Pandas, a popular data manipulation library in Python, to scale and normalize data.

Why do we need to scale and normalize data?

When dealing with machine learning algorithms that use mathematical functions to analyze data, the scale of the input features can significantly impact the model's performance. In particular, algorithms that use distance-based calculations, such as K-Nearest Neighbors and Support Vector Machines, are sensitive to the scale of input features.

Scaling and normalization help to ensure that each feature contributes equally to the analysis and prevent features with larger numerical ranges from dominating the analysis. These techniques can also make the model converge faster during the training process, improving computational efficiency.

Data Scaling Techniques

There are various techniques for scaling data, including:

Standardization

Standardization is the process of transforming data so that it has a mean of 0 and a standard deviation of 1. This can be achieved using the **StandardScaler** class from **sklearn.preprocessing** module.

```
from sklearn.preprocessing import StandardScaler
# create the scaler object
scaler = StandardScaler()
# fit and transform the data
scaled_data = scaler.fit_transform(df[['col1', 'col2', 'col3']])
```

Min-Max Scaling

Min-Max scaling, also known as normalization, scales the data to a range between 0 and 1. This can be done using the **MinMaxScaler** class from **sklearn.preprocessing** module.

```python
from sklearn.preprocessing import MinMaxScaler
# create the scaler object
scaler = MinMaxScaler()
# fit and transform the data
scaled_data = scaler.fit_transform(df[['col1', 'col2', 'col3']])
```

Robust Scaling

Robust scaling is similar to standardization, but instead of using the mean and standard deviation, it uses the median and interquartile range (IQR). This is less sensitive to outliers in the data. This can be done using the **RobustScaler** class from the **sklearn.preprocessing** module.

```python
from sklearn.preprocessing import RobustScaler
# create the scaler object
scaler = RobustScaler()
# fit and transform the data
scaled_data = scaler.fit_transform(df[['col1', 'col2', 'col3']])
```

Log Transformation

Log transformation is used to transform data that has a skewed distribution into a more normal distribution. This can be done using the **numpy** module.

```python
import numpy as np
# log transform the data
transformed_data = np.log(df[['col1', 'col2', 'col3']])
```

Data scaling and normalization are important steps in data

preprocessing for machine learning models. In this section, we have covered various techniques for scaling and normalizing data using the Pandas and Scikit-learn libraries in Python. Understanding these techniques and applying them to your data can help improve the performance of your machine-learning models.

Conclusion

These are just a few examples of the many data cleaning and preprocessing tasks that can be accomplished using Pandas. By mastering these tools, data scientists and analysts can ensure that their data is properly cleaned and prepared for analysis or machine learning.

II.IV Feature engineering

Feature engineering is a crucial step in any machine-learning project. It involves transforming raw data into features that can be used to train a machine-learning model. The goal of feature engineering is to extract the most relevant information from the data and represent it in a way that is suitable for machine learning algorithms.

In Python, there are many libraries available for data manipulation and feature engineering, such as Pandas, NumPy, and Scikit-learn. In this section, we will discuss some of the most commonly used techniques for feature engineering in Python.

1. Handling missing data: One common problem in real-world datasets is missing data. Missing data can be handled in several ways, such as dropping rows or columns with missing values, imputing missing values with mean or median values, or using advanced imputation techniques such as K-nearest neighbors or regression.

Pandas provides several methods for handling missing data, such as **dropna()** to drop rows or columns with missing values, and **fillna()** to fill missing values with a specified value or method.

2. Encoding categorical variables: Categorical variables are variables that take a limited number of values, such as colors or types of cars. These variables cannot be used directly in machine learning algorithms and need to be encoded into numerical values.

Pandas provides several methods for encoding categorical

variables, such as **get_dummies()** for one-hot encoding and **LabelEncoder()** for ordinal encoding.

3. Scaling and normalization: Machine learning algorithms often perform better when the input features are scaled or normalized. Scaling refers to transforming the data to a common scale, such as between 0 and 1 or -1 and 1. Normalization refers to transforming the data to have a mean of 0 and a standard deviation of 1.

Scikit-learn provides several methods for scaling and normalization, such as **MinMaxScaler()** for scaling to a specified range and **StandardScaler()** for normalization.

4. Feature selection: Feature selection involves selecting the most relevant features from the dataset. This can improve the performance of machine learning algorithms and reduce overfitting.

Scikit-learn provides several methods for feature selection, such as **SelectKBest()** for selecting the K best features based on statistical tests and **RFE()** for recursive feature elimination based on the performance of a machine learning model.

5. Feature extraction: Feature extraction involves transforming the raw data into a new set of features that capture the most important information. This can be done using techniques such as Principal Component Analysis (PCA) or Non-negative Matrix Factorization (NMF).

Scikit-learn provides several methods for feature extraction, such as **PCA()** for linear dimensionality reduction and **NMF()** for non-negative matrix factorization.

In conclusion, feature engineering is a crucial step in any machine learning project. Python provides several powerful libraries for data manipulation and feature engineering, such as Pandas, NumPy, and Scikit-learn. By using the techniques discussed in this section, you can transform raw data into features that are suitable for machine learning algorithms and improve the performance of your models.

II.V Data visualization with Matplotlib

Matplotlib is a popular data visualization library in Python that allows users to create a wide range of graphs, charts, and plots to analyze and present data. In this section, we will explore the basics of data visualization with Matplotlib and create some simple visualizations.

Installing Matplotlib

Before we can start using Matplotlib, we need to install it. We can use pip to install Matplotlib with the following command:

```
$ pip install matplotlib
```

Importing Matplotlib

Once Matplotlib is installed, we can import it into our Python code using the following line:

```
$ import matplotlib.pyplot as plt
```

The **pyplot** module of Matplotlib contains many functions that we can use to create different types of plots and customize them as needed.

Line Plot

Let's start with a simple line plot. We'll create a list of x-values and y-values and plot them using the **plot** function.

```
import matplotlib.pyplot as plt
x = [1, 2, 3, 4, 5]
y = [2, 4, 6, 8, 10]
```

```
plt.plot(x, y)
plt.show()
```

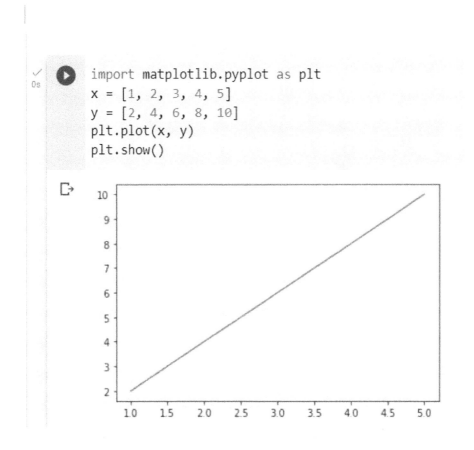

```
import matplotlib.pyplot as plt
x = [1, 2, 3, 4, 5]
y = [2, 4, 6, 8, 10]
plt.plot(x, y)
plt.show()
```

The **plot** function takes two arrays as input, one for the x-axis values and one for the y-axis values. We then use the **show** function to display the plot.

Scatter Plot

We can create a scatter plot using the **scatter** function. Let's plot a set of random points.

```
import matplotlib.pyplot as plt
import random
```

```
x = [random.randint(1, 50) for _ in range(20)]
y = [random.randint(1, 50) for _ in range(20)]
plt.scatter(x, y)
plt.show()
```

```
import matplotlib.pyplot as plt
import random
x = [random.randint(1, 50) for _ in range(20)]
y = [random.randint(1, 50) for _ in range(20)]
plt.scatter(x, y)
plt.show()
```

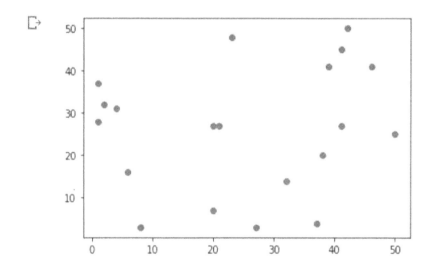

The **scatter** function takes two arrays as input, one for the x-axis values and one for the y-axis values.

Bar Chart

We can create a bar chart using the **bar** function. Let's plot a bar chart for the number of students who prefer different programming languages.

```
import matplotlib.pyplot as plt
languages = ['Python', 'Java', 'C++', 'JavaScript']
students = [40, 30, 25, 5]
plt.bar(languages, students)
plt.show()
```

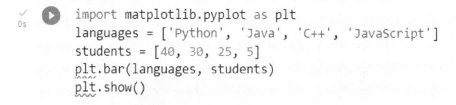

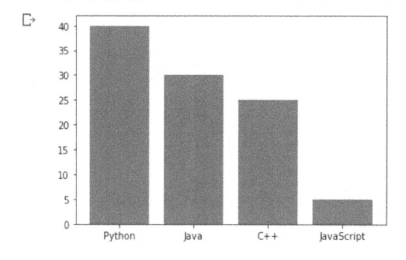

The **bar** function takes two arrays as input, one for the x-axis values and one for the y-axis values.

Histogram

We can create a histogram using the **hist** function. Let's plot a histogram for the ages of a group of people.

import matplotlib.pyplot as plt

ages = [22, 25, 35, 42, 52, 55, 62, 65, 72, 75, 82, 85, 92]

plt.hist(ages, bins=5)

plt.show()

```
import matplotlib.pyplot as plt
ages = [22, 25, 35, 42, 52, 55, 62, 65, 72, 75, 82, 85, 92]
plt.hist(ages, bins=5)
plt.show()
```

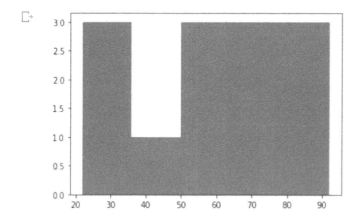

The **hist** function takes an array as input and the number of bins to group the data into.

Customization

Matplotlib offers extensive customization options to make your plots visually appealing and informative. In this section, we will explore some of these options.

Changing Colors and Line Styles

You can change the color and line style of a plot by passing arguments to the **plot** function. For example, to plot a red dashed line, you can use the following code:

```
plt.plot(x, y, color='r', linestyle='--')
```

The **color** argument takes a string that represents a color, such as **'r'** for red, **'g'** for green, **'b'** for blue, and so on. The **linestyle** argument takes a string that represents a line style, such as '-' for a solid line, '--' for a dashed line, ':' for a dotted line, and so on.

Adding Labels and Titles

You can add labels to the x-axis and y-axis using the **xlabel** and **ylabel** functions, respectively. You can also add a title to the plot using the **title** function. For example, the following code adds labels and a title to a plot:

```
plt.plot(x, y)
plt.xlabel('X-axis')
plt.ylabel('Y-axis')
plt.title('My Plot')
```

Adding Legends

If you are plotting multiple lines on the same plot, you can add a legend to differentiate between them. You can do this by giving each line a label using the **label** argument and then calling the **legend** function. For example:

```
plt.plot(x, y1, label='Line 1')
plt.plot(x, y2, label='Line 2')
plt.legend()
```

Changing Font Sizes

You can change the font size of the plot labels and title using the **fontsize** argument. For example:

```
plt.plot(x, y)
plt.xlabel('X-axis', fontsize=16)
plt.ylabel('Y-axis', fontsize=16)
plt.title('My Plot', fontsize=20)
```

Changing Ticks and Tick Labels

You can change the ticks and tick labels of the plot using the **xticks** and **yticks** functions. For example, the following code sets the x-axis ticks to be at **[0, 1, 2, 3, 4]** and sets the y-axis ticks to be at **[0, 2, 4, 6, 8]**:

```
plt.plot(x, y)
plt.xticks([0, 1, 2, 3, 4])
plt.yticks([0, 2, 4, 6, 8])
```

You can also change the tick label text by passing a list of strings to the **xticklabels** and **yticklabels** functions. For example:

```
plt.plot(x, y)
plt.xticks([0, 1, 2, 3, 4], ['Jan', 'Feb', 'Mar', 'Apr', 'May'])
plt.yticks([0, 2, 4, 6, 8], ['0', '2K', '4K', '6K', '8K'])
```

Changing Plot Size and Resolution

Matplotlib allows you to control the size of your plots by specifying the **figsize** parameter when creating a new figure. For example, the following code will create a figure with a width of 8 inches and a height of 6 inches:

```
import matplotlib.pyplot as plt
fig = plt.figure(figsize=(8, 6))
```

You can also change the resolution of your plots by specifying the **dpi** parameter. The default resolution is 100 dpi, but you can increase this value to create higher-resolution plots. For example, the following code will create a figure with a resolution of 200 dpi:

```
fig = plt.figure(figsize=(8, 6), dpi=200)
```

Customizing Colors and Styles

Matplotlib allows you to customize the colors and styles of your plots in a variety of ways. Here are a few examples:

- **Changing the line color:** You can change the color of a line by specifying the **color** parameter. For example, the following code will create a red line:

  pythonCopy code

  ```
  plt.plot(x, y, color='red')
  ```

- **Changing the line style:** You can change the style of a line by specifying the **linestyle** parameter. For example, the following code will create a dashed line:

  ```
  plt.plot(x, y, linestyle='--')
  ```

- **Changing the marker style:** You can add markers to your plot by specifying the **marker** parameter. For example, the following code will create a plot with circular markers:

  ```
  plt.plot(x, y, marker='o')
  ```

- **Changing the fill style:** You can change the fill style of markers by specifying the **markerfacecolor** parameter. For example, the following code will create a plot with blue-filled markers:

  ```
  plt.plot(x, y, marker='o', markerfacecolor='blue')
  ```

- **Changing the font size:** You can change the font size of the text in your plots by specifying the **fontsize** parameter. For example, the following code will create a plot with larger font:

```
plt.xlabel('x-axis',      fontsize=16)      plt.ylabel('y-axis',
fontsize=16) plt.title('Title', fontsize=18)
```

These are just a few examples of the many ways you can customize the colors and styles of your plots in Matplotlib.

Conclusion

Matplotlib is a powerful data visualization library for Python that allows you to create a wide range of plots, from simple line plots to complex 3D visualizations. In this section, we covered the basics of creating plots with Matplotlib, including how to create line plots, scatter plots, and histograms, and how to customize the appearance of your plots. With this knowledge, you should be able to create a wide range of plots for your data science projects.

III. SUPERVISED LEARNING WITH SCIKIT-LEARN

Machine learning is a branch of artificial intelligence that allows computers to learn from data without being explicitly programmed. One of the most popular areas of machine learning is supervised learning, which involves training a machine learning model on a labeled dataset to make predictions on new, unseen data. Scikit-learn is a powerful Python library that provides a wide range of tools for supervised learning tasks such as regression and classification. In this chapter, we will explore some of the key concepts of supervised learning and learn how to use scikit-learn to build and evaluate predictive models.

III.I Overview of the Scikit-learn library

Scikit-learn is one of the most popular Python libraries for machine learning. It is built on top of NumPy, SciPy, and matplotlib, and it provides a simple and efficient tool for data mining and data analysis. Scikit-learn is easy to use and has a comprehensive set of tools for supervised and unsupervised learning tasks, including classification, regression, clustering, and dimensionality reduction.

Scikit-learn provides a range of supervised and unsupervised learning algorithms and tools for model selection and evaluation. Some of the key features of Scikit-learn include:

1. Simple and consistent API: Scikit-learn provides a consistent interface for working with a range of machine learning models, making it easy to switch between models and compare their performance.

2. Built-in datasets: Scikit-learn includes several real-world datasets that can be used for testing and experimentation.

3. Feature extraction and selection: Scikit-learn includes tools for feature extraction and selection, which can be used to identify the most important features in a dataset.

4. Model selection and evaluation: Scikit-learn includes tools for model selection and evaluation, such as cross-validation and grid search.

5. Support for parallel processing: Scikit-learn supports parallel processing, which can speed up the training and evaluation of machine learning models.

In the next sections, we will explore some of the key features of Scikit-learn and demonstrate how to use them for common machine-learning tasks.

III.II Linear Regression

Linear regression is a popular technique for modeling and analyzing data. It is a method for predicting a dependent variable (also known as a response variable) based on one or more independent variables (also known as predictor variables or features). In this section, we will use the Scikit-learn library to build a simple linear regression model.

Importing Required Libraries

We will start by importing the necessary libraries. We will use numpy for numerical computations and matplotlib for visualization. We will also import the LinearRegression class from the Scikit-learn library.

```
import numpy as np
import matplotlib.pyplot as plt
from sklearn.linear_model import LinearRegression
```

Generating Data

Next, we will generate some synthetic data to work with. We will create a simple dataset with one feature (x) and a dependent variable (y) that is linearly related to the feature. We will add some random noise to the data to make it more realistic.

```
# Generate random data
np.random.seed(0)
n_samples = 100
X = np.linspace(0, 10, n_samples)[:, np.newaxis]
y = X + np.random.randn(n_samples, 1)
```

Plotting the Data

Before we proceed with the model fitting, let's visualize the data.

```
# Plot the data
plt.scatter(X, y, color='black')
plt.xlabel('X')
plt.ylabel('Y')
plt.show()
```

This will create a scatter plot of the data.

```
import numpy as np
import matplotlib.pyplot as plt
from sklearn.linear_model import LinearRegression

# Generate random data
np.random.seed(0)
n_samples = 100
X = np.linspace(0, 10, n_samples)[:, np.newaxis]
y = X + np.random.randn(n_samples, 1)

# Plot the data
plt.scatter(X, y, color='black')
plt.xlabel('X')
plt.ylabel('Y')
plt.show()
```

Fitting the Model

Now, let's fit a linear regression model to the data. We will create an instance of the LinearRegression class and call its fit() method to fit the model.

```
# Fit linear regression model
model = LinearRegression()
model.fit(X, y)
```

Visualizing the Results

Once the model is fitted, we can visualize the results by plotting the regression line. We can use the predict() method of the model to generate predictions for the range of values in the dataset, and then plot the predicted values against the original data.

```
# Predict values
y_pred = model.predict(X)
# Plot the linear regression line
plt.scatter(X, y, color='black')
plt.plot(X, y_pred, color='blue', linewidth=3)
plt.xlabel('X')
plt.ylabel('Y')
plt.show()
```

This will create a plot with the regression line.

```
# Fit linear regression model
model = LinearRegression()
model.fit(X, y)

# Predict values
y_pred = model.predict(X)

# Plot the linear regression line
plt.scatter(X, y, color='black')
plt.plot(X, y_pred, color='blue', linewidth=3)
plt.xlabel('X')
plt.ylabel('Y')
plt.show()
```

Conclusion

In this section, we used Scikit-learn to build a simple linear regression model. We generated some synthetic data, visualized it, fitted a linear regression model to it, and then visualized the results. Linear regression is just one of the many techniques that Scikit-learn provides. Scikit-learn is a powerful library for machine learning that provides a wide range of tools and algorithms for data analysis and modeling.

III.III Logistic Regression

Logistic regression is a popular algorithm used for classification tasks in machine learning. It is a simple yet powerful algorithm that can be used for both binary and multiclass classification problems. Logistic regression models the probability of a certain outcome by fitting a logistic function to the input features. In this section, we will learn how to implement logistic regression using scikit-learn.

Dataset

We will be using the famous Iris flower dataset for this section. This dataset contains 150 samples of three different species of Iris flowers (Setosa, Versicolor, and Virginica). For each sample, we have four features: sepal length, sepal width, petal length, and petal width. Our task is to classify the flowers into their respective species based on these features.

We will load the dataset using scikit-learn's **load_iris()** function:

```
from sklearn.datasets import load_iris
iris = load_iris()
X = iris.data
y = iris.target
```

Data Splitting

Before we start training our model, we need to split our data into training and testing sets. This is important to ensure that our model does not overfit the training data and generalizes well to new, unseen data.

We will split the data into 80% training and 20% testing using scikit-learn's **train_test_split()** function:

```
from sklearn.model_selection import train_test_split
X_train, X_test, y_train, y_test = train_test_split(X, y,
test_size=0.2, random_state=42)
```

Model Training

Now we can train our logistic regression model using scikit-learn's **LogisticRegression()** class:

```
from sklearn.linear_model import LogisticRegression
clf = LogisticRegression(random_state=42)
clf.fit(X_train, y_train)
```

Model Evaluation

Once we have trained our model, we can evaluate its performance on the test set using scikit-learn's **accuracy_score()** function:

```
from sklearn.metrics import accuracy_score
y_pred = clf.predict(X_test)
accuracy = accuracy_score(y_test, y_pred)
print("Accuracy:", accuracy)
```

The accuracy of our model on the test set should be around 0.9667.

```
# Dataset
from sklearn.datasets import load_iris
iris = load_iris()
X = iris.data
y = iris.target

# Data Splitting
from sklearn.model_selection import train_test_split
X_train, X_test, y_train, y_test = train_test_split(X, y, test_size=0.2, random_state=42)

# Model Training
from sklearn.linear_model import LogisticRegression
clf = LogisticRegression(random_state=42)
clf.fit(X_train, y_train)

# Model Evaluation
from sklearn.metrics import accuracy_score
y_pred = clf.predict(X_test)
accuracy = accuracy_score(y_test, y_pred)
print("Accuracy:", accuracy)
```

```
Accuracy: 1.0
```

Conclusion

Logistic regression is a simple and effective algorithm for classification tasks. In this section, we learned how to implement logistic regression using scikit-learn and applied it to the Iris flower dataset. We also learned how to split our data into training and testing sets, and how to evaluate the performance of our model using an accuracy score. Scikit-learn provides many other algorithms and evaluation metrics for classification tasks, which we can explore in future sections.

III.IV Decision Trees and Random Forests

Decision Trees and Random Forests are two popular machine-learning algorithms for classification and regression problems. They are easy to use and interpret, making them a popular choice among data scientists. In this section, we will cover how to use Scikit-learn's implementation of Decision Trees and Random Forests for both classification and regression problems.

Prerequisites

To follow along with this section, you should have some knowledge of Python and machine learning concepts. Specifically, you should be familiar with Scikit-learn and its basic functionality.

Dataset

We will use the famous iris dataset for classification and the Boston Housing dataset for regression. Scikit-learn provides these datasets, so there is no need to download them separately.

Decision Trees

Decision Trees are a simple yet powerful machine learning algorithm that can be used for both classification and regression tasks. They work by recursively splitting the data based on the features that provide the most information gain. The result is a tree-like structure where each internal node represents a decision based on a feature, and each leaf node represents a class label or a numerical value.

Training a Decision Tree Classifier

To train a Decision Tree Classifier, we will use the iris dataset. We will first load the dataset using Scikit-learn's **load_iris()** function:

```
from sklearn.datasets import load_iris
iris = load_iris()
```

Next, we will split the dataset into training and testing sets:

```
from sklearn.model_selection import train_test_split
X_train, X_test, y_train, y_test = train_test_split(iris.data, iris.target, test_size=0.3, random_state=42)
```

Now, we can create and train the Decision Tree Classifier using Scikit-learn's **DecisionTreeClassifier** class:

```
from sklearn.tree import DecisionTreeClassifier
dt = DecisionTreeClassifier()
dt.fit(X_train, y_train)
```

That's it! Our Decision Tree Classifier is now trained and ready to make predictions. We can evaluate its performance on the testing set using Scikit-learn's **accuracy_score** function:

```
from sklearn.metrics import accuracy_score
y_pred = dt.predict(X_test)
print("Accuracy:", accuracy_score(y_test, y_pred))
```

Visualizing the Decision Tree

We can also visualize the Decision Tree using Scikit-learn's **export_graphviz** function and Graphviz software. Here's how:

```
from sklearn.tree import export_graphviz
export_graphviz(dt, out_file='tree.dot',
feature_names=iris.feature_names,
class_names=iris.target_names, filled=True)
```

```
# Load the dataset
from sklearn.datasets import load_iris
iris = load_iris()

# Split the dataset
from sklearn.model_selection import train_test_split
X_train, X_test, y_train, y_test = train_test_split(iris.data, iris.target, test_size=0.3, random_state=42)

# Can create and train the Decision Tree Classifier
from sklearn.tree import DecisionTreeClassifier
dt = DecisionTreeClassifier()
dt.fit(X_train, y_train)

# Evaluate the performance on the testing set
from sklearn.metrics import accuracy_score
y_pred = dt.predict(X_test)
print("Accuracy:", accuracy_score(y_test, y_pred))

# Visualizing the Decision Tree
from sklearn.tree import export_graphviz
export_graphviz(dt, out_file='tree.dot', feature_names=iris.feature_names, class_names=iris.target_names, filled=True)
```

```
Accuracy: 1.0
```

This will create a file called **tree.dot** in the current directory. To convert it to a PNG image, we need to use Graphviz software. You can download it from the official website: https://graphviz.org/download/. Once installed, we can run the following command in the terminal:

$ dot -Tpng tree.dot -o tree.png

```
[16] !ls

        sample_data    tree.dot
```

```
[20] !dot -Tpng tree.dot -o tree.png
```

```
[21] !ls

        sample_data    tree.dot    tree.png
```

This will create a PNG image called **tree.png** in the current directory. To display the .png image use:

```
from IPython.display import Image
Image('tree.png')
```

Here's what the Decision Tree looks like:

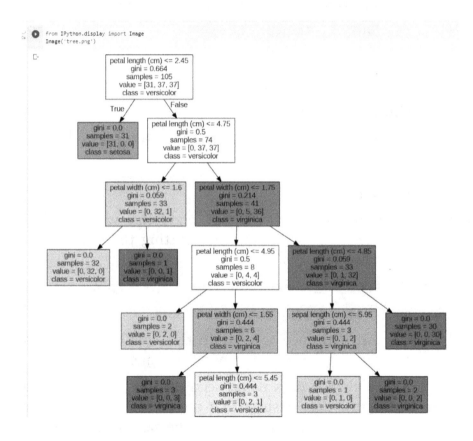

Training a Decision Tree Regressor

In addition to classification problems, decision trees can also be used for regression tasks. In this section, we'll train a decision tree regressor on a dataset of house prices.

Dataset

The dataset we'll be using is the California Housing dataset, which contains information about the median house price, total rooms, total bedrooms, population, households, median income, and latitude/longitude for various districts in California. We'll load the dataset using scikit-learn's **fetch_california_housing()** function.

```
from sklearn.datasets import fetch_california_housing
# Load the California Housing dataset
california = fetch_california_housing()
# Print the dataset description
print(california.DESCR)
```

The output will describe the dataset and its features.

Preprocessing

Before training the decision tree regressor, we'll need to preprocess the data. We'll start by splitting the dataset into training and test sets.

```
from sklearn.model_selection import train_test_split
# Split the dataset into training and test sets
X_train, X_test, y_train, y_test = train_test_split(california.data, california.target, test_size=0.2, random_state=42)
```

Next, we'll scale the data using scikit-learn's **StandardScaler** class. Scaling the data ensures that each feature has a similar range of values, which can improve the performance of the decision tree regressor.

```
from sklearn.preprocessing import StandardScaler
# Scale the training data
scaler = StandardScaler()
```

```
X_train_scaled = scaler.fit_transform(X_train)
# Scale the test data using the same scaler
X_test_scaled = scaler.transform(X_test)
```

Training the Decision Tree Regressor

With the data preprocessed, we can now train the decision tree regressor. We'll use scikit-learn's **DecisionTreeRegressor** class, which works similarly to the **DecisionTreeClassifier** class we used earlier.

```
from sklearn.tree import DecisionTreeRegressor
# Train a decision tree regressor
dt_reg = DecisionTreeRegressor(random_state=42)
dt_reg.fit(X_train_scaled, y_train)
```

Evaluating the Model

To evaluate the performance of the decision tree regressor, we'll use the mean squared error (MSE) and the coefficient of determination (R^2 score).

```
from sklearn.metrics import mean_squared_error, r2_score
# Predict the test set
y_pred = dt_reg.predict(X_test_scaled)
# Calculate the mean squared error and the R^2 score
mse = mean_squared_error(y_test, y_pred)
r2 = r2_score(y_test, y_pred)
print(f"Mean squared error: {mse:.2f}")
print(f"R^2 score: {r2:.2f}")
```

The output will show the mean squared error and the R^2 score of the model.

Visualizing the Decision Tree

We can visualize the decision tree using scikit-learn's **plot_tree()** function. This function generates a plot of the decision tree, which can be useful for understanding how the model is making its predictions.

```
from sklearn.tree import plot_tree
# Plot the decision tree
plot_tree(dt_reg)
```

The output will be a visualization of the decision tree.

Conclusion

We covered the basic concepts of decision trees, how to train and visualize a decision tree, and how to improve its performance using ensemble methods such as random forests. We also went over how to evaluate a model's performance and make predictions on new data.

Decision trees and random forests are powerful and widely used machine learning techniques that can be applied to a variety of problems, from regression to classification tasks. However, they do have limitations, such as overfitting, and it is important to carefully select and preprocess the data and tune the model's hyperparameters to achieve the best results.

III.V Support Vector Machines

Support Vector Machines (SVMs) are a type of supervised machine learning algorithm used for classification and regression analysis. SVMs can be used to analyze data for both linear and non-linear relationships. They are powerful algorithms that can be used for both classification and regression problems, and they can handle large datasets.

The main idea behind SVMs is to find a hyperplane that maximally separates the different classes in the data. In the case of non-linearly separable data, SVMs use a kernel function to transform the data into a higher-dimensional space where it is linearly separable.

Scikit-learn provides an implementation of SVMs that is easy to use and highly customizable.

Setting up the Data

To demonstrate how to use scikit-learn's SVM implementation, we will use the well-known Iris dataset. The Iris dataset is a classic example of a dataset for classification tasks. It consists of measurements of the sepal length, sepal width, petal length, and petal width of three different species of iris flowers: Setosa, Versicolor, and Virginica.

To begin, we will import the necessary libraries and load the dataset:

```python
import numpy as np
import matplotlib.pyplot as plt
from sklearn import datasets
from sklearn.model_selection import train_test_split
from sklearn import svm
```

```
# Load the Iris dataset
iris = datasets.load_iris()
# Extract the features and labels
X = iris.data[:, :2]  # we only take the first two features.
y = iris.target
# Split the data into training and test sets
X_train, X_test, y_train, y_test = train_test_split(X, y,
test_size=0.3, random_state=42)
```

Here, we use the **load_iris** function from scikit-learn's **datasets** module to load the dataset. We extract the first two features of the dataset (**sepal length** and **sepal width**) and the corresponding labels. We then split the data into training and test sets using the **train_test_split** function.

Training an SVM Model

To train an SVM model, we first create an instance of the **svm.SVC** class, which stands for Support Vector Classification. We can then fit the model to our training data using the **fit** method.

```
# Create an SVM classifier with a linear kernel
clf = svm.SVC(kernel='linear')
# Train the classifier on the training data
clf.fit(X_train, y_train)
```

Here, we create an instance of the **svm.SVC** class with a linear kernel and call it **clf**. We then fit the model to our training data using the **fit** method.

Making Predictions

Once the model is trained, we can use it to make predictions on new data using the **predict** method.

```
# Make predictions on the test data
y_pred = clf.predict(X_test)
```

Here, we use the **predict** method to make predictions on our test data.

Evaluating the Model

To evaluate the performance of our SVM model, we can use several metrics, such as accuracy, precision, and recall. Scikit-learn provides a convenient **classification_report** function that calculates these metrics for us.

```
from sklearn.metrics import classification_report
# Print the classification report
print(classification_report(y_test, y_pred))
```

Here, we import the **classification_report** function from scikit-learn's **metrics** module and use it to print a report of the classification metrics.

Visualizing the Results

To better understand how the SVM classifier is performing, let's visualize the results using the **matplotlib** library. We can plot the decision boundary and the support vectors on a 2D plot.

```
# Plot the decision boundary
plt.scatter(X[:, 0], X[:, 1], c=y, cmap='winter')
ax = plt.gca()
xlim = ax.get_xlim()
ylim = ax.get_ylim()
xx = np.linspace(xlim[0], xlim[1], 30)
yy = np.linspace(ylim[0], ylim[1], 30)
YY, XX = np.meshgrid(yy, xx)
```

```
xy = np.vstack([XX.ravel(), YY.ravel()]).T
Z = svm.decision_function(xy).reshape(XX.shape)
ax.contour(XX, YY, Z, colors='k', levels=[-1, 0, 1], alpha=0.5,
    linestyles=['--', '-', '--'])
ax.scatter(svm.support_vectors_[:, 0], svm.support_vectors_[:,
1], s=100,
    linewidth=1, facecolors='none', edgecolors='k')
plt.show()
```

The above code will plot the decision boundary as well as the support vectors on the plot. The **scatter()** function is used to plot the input data. We use **get_xlim()** and **get_ylim()** methods to get the minimum and maximum values of the X and Y axes, respectively. We then create a meshgrid using **linspace()** function and pass it to **decision_function()** to get the decision boundary values. Finally, we plot the decision boundary using **contour()** and the support vectors using **scatter()**.

The resulting plot should look like this:

The decision boundary is shown as a solid black line, while the dashed lines represent the margin of the classifier. The support vectors are represented as black circles. As we can see, the SVM classifier does a good job of separating the two classes and the decision boundary is linear.

Conclusion

In this section, we learned about the Support Vector Machine (SVM) algorithm and how to use it for classification problems using scikit-learn library in Python. SVM is a powerful and versatile machine-learning algorithm that can be used for a wide range of applications, including image classification, text classification, and speech recognition. By experimenting with different kernel functions, we can achieve a higher accuracy for our classification problem. We also saw how to visualize the decision boundary and the support vectors using the matplotlib library.

III.VI K-Nearest Neighbors

K-Nearest Neighbors (KNN) is a machine learning algorithm that is commonly used for classification and regression tasks. In this section, we will explore how to use the Scikit-learn library to implement KNN for classification tasks.

Understanding KNN

KNN is a simple but effective machine-learning algorithm. The basic idea behind KNN is to classify a new data point by finding the K closest data points in the training set and then taking the majority class of those K points as the predicted class for the new data point.

The K in KNN represents the number of closest data points we want to consider. A larger value of K will result in a smoother decision boundary and a smaller value of K will result in a more complex decision boundary.

KNN is a non-parametric algorithm, which means it does not make any assumptions about the underlying distribution of the data. It is also a lazy learning algorithm, which means it does not actually learn a model from the training data but instead stores the entire training dataset.

Implementation of KNN in Scikit-learn

We will use the Iris dataset for this section, which is a well-known dataset in the machine learning community. The Iris dataset contains 150 samples of iris flowers, with 50 samples from each of three different species. Each sample contains four features: sepal length, sepal width, petal length, and petal width.

First, we will import the necessary libraries:

```
import numpy as np
import matplotlib.pyplot as plt
from sklearn.datasets import load_iris
from sklearn.neighbors import KNeighborsClassifier
from sklearn.model_selection import train_test_split
from sklearn.metrics import accuracy_score
```

Next, we will load the Iris dataset and split it into training and testing sets:

```
iris = load_iris()
X_train, X_test, y_train, y_test = train_test_split(iris.data, iris.target, test_size=0.3, random_state=42)
```

In the above code, we split the dataset into 70% training data and 30% testing data.

Next, we will create an instance of the KNeighborsClassifier class and fit it to the training data:

```
knn = KNeighborsClassifier(n_neighbors=3)
knn.fit(X_train, y_train)
```

In the above code, we create an instance of the KNeighborsClassifier class with K=3 and then fit it to the training data.

Next, we will make predictions on the testing data:

```
y_pred = knn.predict(X_test)
```

Finally, we will evaluate the accuracy of the model:

```
accuracy = accuracy_score(y_test, y_pred)
print('Accuracy:', accuracy)
```

Conclusion

K-Nearest Neighbors is a simple but powerful machine learning algorithm. In this section, we learned how to implement KNN in

Scikit-learn for classification tasks. We also saw how to evaluate the accuracy of the model using the accuracy_score function.

III.VII Naive Bayes

Naive Bayes is a classification algorithm based on Bayes' theorem, which assumes that the presence of a particular feature in a class is unrelated to the presence of any other feature. This is known as the "naive" assumption, which makes the algorithm simple and fast, yet effective for many real-world problems.

In scikit-learn, there are several types of Naive Bayes classifiers available, including Gaussian Naive Bayes, Multinomial Naive Bayes, and Bernoulli Naive Bayes. In this section, we'll focus on Gaussian Naive Bayes, which is suitable for continuous input variables.

Dataset

For this section, we'll use the famous Iris dataset, which contains measurements of iris flowers along with their species. The goal is to predict the species of an iris flower based on its measurements.

Let's start by loading the dataset and splitting it into training and testing sets.

```python
from sklearn.datasets import load_iris
from sklearn.model_selection import train_test_split
# Load the dataset
iris = load_iris()
# Split the dataset into training and testing sets
X_train, X_test, y_train, y_test = train_test_split(iris.data, iris.target, test_size=0.3, random_state=42)
```

Gaussian Naive Bayes Classifier

To train a Gaussian Naive Bayes classifier in scikit-learn, we first need to import the **GaussianNB** class from the **sklearn.naive_bayes** module.

```
from sklearn.naive_bayes import GaussianNB
# Create a Gaussian Naive Bayes classifier
clf = GaussianNB()
# Train the classifier on the training data
clf.fit(X_train, y_train)
```

Evaluating the Model

Once we've trained the classifier, we can use it to make predictions on the testing set and evaluate its performance using various metrics. In this example, we'll use accuracy as the evaluation metric.

```
from sklearn.metrics import accuracy_score
# Make predictions on the testing data
y_pred = clf.predict(X_test)
# Evaluate the model's accuracy
accuracy = accuracy_score(y_test, y_pred)
print("Accuracy:", accuracy)
```

Conclusion

In this section, we learned how to use the Gaussian Naive Bayes algorithm in scikit-learn for classification tasks. We also evaluated the performance of the model using the accuracy metric. Naive Bayes is a simple yet powerful algorithm that can be effective in many real-world scenarios, especially when dealing with high-dimensional datasets.

III.VIII Model Evaluation and Metrics

Scikit-learn provides a variety of metrics for evaluating the performance of machine learning models. These metrics are used to assess the accuracy, precision, recall, and F1 score of the model, among others. In this section, we will go through some of the most commonly used evaluation metrics and how to use them in Scikit-learn.

Confusion Matrix

A confusion matrix is a table that is used to evaluate the performance of a classification model. It shows the number of true positives, true negatives, false positives, and false negatives for a given model. Scikit-learn provides a function **confusion_matrix** that can be used to generate the confusion matrix for a given set of predictions and true labels.

```
from sklearn.metrics import confusion_matrix
y_true = [0, 1, 0, 1, 0, 1, 0, 1, 1, 1]
y_pred = [0, 1, 0, 1, 1, 1, 0, 0, 1, 0]
confusion_matrix(y_true, y_pred)
```

This will output:

```
array([[3, 1],
       [2, 4]])
```

In this example, the confusion matrix shows that the model correctly classified 3 instances as true negatives and 4 instances as true positives. It also incorrectly classified 1 instance as a false negative and 2 instances as false positives.

Accuracy

Accuracy is a metric that measures the overall performance of a classification model. It is defined as the number of correct predictions divided by the total number of predictions. Scikit-learn provides a function **accuracy_score** that can be used to calculate the accuracy of a given set of predictions and true labels.

```
from sklearn.metrics import accuracy_score
accuracy_score(y_true, y_pred)
```

This will output:

```
0.7
```

In this example, the accuracy of the model is 0.7 or 70%.

Precision, Recall, and F1 Score

Precision, recall, and F1 score are metrics that are commonly used in machine learning to evaluate the performance of a classification model. Precision measures the fraction of true positives among the instances that the model classified as positive. Recall measures the fraction of true positives that the model correctly classified as positive. The F1 score is the harmonic mean of precision and recall.

Scikit-learn provides functions **precision_score**, **recall_score**, and **f1_score** that can be used to calculate these metrics for a given set of predictions and true labels.

```
from sklearn.metrics import precision_score, recall_score, f1_score
precision_score(y_true, y_pred)
```

This will output:

```
0.8
```

```
recall_score(y_true, y_pred)
```

This will output:

```
0.6666666666666666
```

f1_score(y_true, y_pred)

This will output:

```
0.7272727272727273
```

In this example, the precision of the model is 0.8, the recall is 0.6667, and the F1 score is 0.7273.

ROC Curve

Another commonly used metric for evaluating binary classification models is the receiver operating characteristic (ROC) curve. The ROC curve is a plot of the true positive rate (TPR) versus the false positive rate (FPR) for different classification thresholds.

To generate the ROC curve, we need to compute the TPR and FPR for various threshold values. The TPR is also known as sensitivity or recall, and it is defined as the number of true positives divided by the sum of true positives and false negatives. The FPR, on the other hand, is defined as the number of false positives divided by the sum of false positives and true negatives.

Scikit-learn provides a convenient function, **roc_curve()**, for computing the TPR and FPR at different threshold values. Here's an example:

from sklearn.metrics import roc_curve

fpr, tpr, thresholds = roc_curve(y_test, y_pred_prob[:,1])

Here, **y_test** is the true class labels of the test set, and **y_pred_prob[:,1]** is the predicted probability of the positive class (i.e., class 1) from our model.

The **roc_curve()** function returns three arrays: **fpr**, **tpr**, and **thresholds**. The **fpr** and **tpr** arrays contain the FPR and TPR at different threshold values, and the **thresholds** array contains the corresponding threshold values.

We can plot the ROC curve using Matplotlib as follows:

```
import matplotlib.pyplot as plt
plt.plot(fpr, tpr)
plt.xlabel('False Positive Rate')
plt.ylabel('True Positive Rate')
plt.title('ROC Curve')
plt.show()
```

The resulting plot is the ROC curve for our model. The closer the curve is to the upper left corner of the plot, the better the model's performance. We can also compute the area under the ROC curve (AUC), which is a single number that summarizes the overall performance of the model. Scikit-learn provides a function, **roc_auc_score()**, for computing the AUC:

```
from sklearn.metrics import roc_auc_score
auc = roc_auc_score(y_test, y_pred_prob[:,1])
print('AUC:', auc)
```

Here, **y_test** and **y_pred_prob[:,1]** are the same as in the **roc_curve()** example above.

The **roc_auc_score()** function returns the AUC for our model. A perfect classifier has an AUC of 1, while a random classifier has an AUC of 0.5. Therefore, the closer the AUC is to 1, the better the model's performance.

In summary, the ROC curve and AUC are useful tools for evaluating binary classification models. They provide a visual representation of the trade-off between the true positive rate and the false positive rate at different classification thresholds and a single number that summarizes the overall performance of the model.

IV. UNSUPERVISED LEARNING WITH SCIKIT-LEARN

U nsupervised learning is a type of machine learning that involves finding patterns or structures in data without any prior knowledge of what those patterns might be. In contrast to supervised learning, where the algorithm is trained on labeled data to predict outcomes for new, unseen data, unsupervised learning algorithms are used for tasks such as clustering and dimensionality reduction. Scikit-learn provides a variety of tools and algorithms for unsupervised learning, making it a powerful library for exploring and analyzing data. In this chapter, we will cover some of the most common unsupervised learning techniques available in scikit-learn, including clustering with k-means and hierarchical clustering, and dimensionality reduction with principal component analysis (PCA) and t-distributed stochastic neighbor embedding (t-SNE).

IV.I Clustering with K-Means and Hierarchical Clustering

Clustering is a type of unsupervised learning that involves grouping similar data points based on certain characteristics or features. The goal of clustering is to identify patterns or structures within the data that may not be immediately apparent. In this section, we will explore two common clustering algorithms: K-Means and Hierarchical Clustering, using the Scikit-learn library in Python.

Installing Scikit-learn

Before we start, let's make sure we have Scikit-learn installed. You can install Scikit-learn using pip, by running the following command in your terminal:

```
$ pip install scikit-learn
```

K-Means Clustering

K-Means is a popular clustering algorithm that aims to partition a dataset into K clusters, where each cluster represents a distinct group of data points. The algorithm works by iteratively assigning data points to the nearest cluster center (centroid) based on their distance and updating the centroids to reflect the mean of the assigned data points.

To illustrate how K-Means works, let's generate a simple dataset with two clusters:

```
import numpy as np
from sklearn.datasets import make_blobs
import matplotlib.pyplot as plt
# Generate a dataset with two clusters
```

```
X,     y     =     make_blobs(n_samples=100,     centers=2,
random_state=42)
# Visualize the dataset
plt.scatter(X[:, 0], X[:, 1])
plt.xlabel('Feature 1')
plt.ylabel('Feature 2')
plt.show()
```

The above code will generate a scatter plot of the dataset with two clusters. We can see that there are two distinct groups of data points.

Now, let's use the K-Means algorithm to cluster the data:

```
from sklearn.cluster import KMeans
# Initialize the K-Means algorithm with K=2
kmeans = KMeans(n_clusters=2)
# Fit the K-Means algorithm to the data
kmeans.fit(X)
# Get the cluster assignments for each data point
y_pred = kmeans.predict(X)
# Visualize the clustering result
plt.scatter(X[:, 0], X[:, 1], c=y_pred)
plt.xlabel('Feature 1')
plt.ylabel('Feature 2')
plt.show()
```

The above code will cluster the data into two groups and produce a scatter plot where each point is colored according to its assigned cluster. We can see that the K-Means algorithm has successfully separated the two clusters.

Hierarchical Clustering

Hierarchical Clustering, also known as agglomerative clustering, is another type of clustering algorithm that groups similar data points in a hierarchical manner. It starts with each data point as a separate cluster and gradually merges the clusters until only one cluster remains. Hierarchical clustering can be represented using a dendrogram, which is a tree-like diagram that shows the order and distances of cluster merges.

Scikit-learn provides an implementation of hierarchical clustering in the **AgglomerativeClustering** class. Let's see how we can use this class to cluster our data.

Hierarchical Clustering with Scikit-learn

First, let's generate some data to work with. We will use the **make_blobs** function from scikit-learn to create a dataset with three blobs.

```python
from sklearn.datasets import make_blobs
import matplotlib.pyplot as plt
# Generate some data
X, y = make_blobs(n_samples=300, centers=3, cluster_std=0.5,
random_state=0)
# Plot the data
plt.scatter(X[:, 0], X[:, 1], s=50)
plt.show()
```

This will generate a dataset with three blobs that are separated:

+ Code + Text

```
from sklearn.datasets import make_blobs
import matplotlib.pyplot as plt

# Generate some data
X, y = make_blobs(n_samples=300, centers=3, cluster_std=0.5, random_state=0)
# Plot the data
plt.scatter(X[:, 0], X[:, 1], s=50)
plt.show()
```

Now let's use the **AgglomerativeClustering** class to cluster this data. We will start with a small number of clusters and gradually increase it to see how the clustering changes.

from sklearn.cluster import AgglomerativeClustering

Perform hierarchical clustering with varying numbers of clusters

for n_clusters in range(2, 6):

  # Create an instance of AgglomerativeClustering with the specified number of clusters

  clustering = AgglomerativeClustering(n_clusters=n_clusters)

  # Fit the model to the data

  clustering.fit(X)

  # Plot the data with colors according to the cluster assignments

```
plt.scatter(X[:, 0], X[:, 1], c=clustering.labels_, cmap='rainbow',
s=50)
```

```
plt.title(f"{n_clusters} Clusters")
```

plt.show()

This will create a plot for each number of clusters, showing the data points with colors according to their cluster assignments:

```
from sklearn.cluster import AgglomerativeClustering

# Perform hierarchical clustering with varying numbers of clusters
for n_clusters in range(2, 6):
    # Create an instance of AgglomerativeClustering with the specified number of clusters
    clustering = AgglomerativeClustering(n_clusters=n_clusters)
    # Fit the model to the data
    clustering.fit(X)
    # Plot the data with colors according to the cluster assignments
    plt.scatter(X[:, 0], X[:, 1], c=clustering.labels_, cmap='rainbow', s=50)
    plt.title(f"{n_clusters} Clusters")
    plt.show()
```

As you can see, the clustering algorithm correctly identifies the three blobs in the data, even when we use a small number of clusters. The dendrogram representation of the hierarchical clustering can be obtained using the **scipy** library and its **dendrogram** function. Here's how you can plot the dendrogram:

from scipy.cluster.hierarchy import dendrogram, linkage

Compute the linkage matrix

Z = linkage(X, method='ward')

```
# Plot the dendrogram
dendrogram(Z)
plt.show()
```

This will create a dendrogram that shows the order and distances of cluster merges:

```
from scipy.cluster.hierarchy import dendrogram, linkage

# Compute the linkage matrix
Z = linkage(X, method='ward')

# Plot the dendrogram
dendrogram(Z)
plt.show()
```

This dendrogram can be useful to visualize the hierarchy of the clusters and to choose an appropriate number of clusters.

Conclusion

In this section, we learned about clustering algorithms and

how to implement K-Means and hierarchical clustering using scikit-learn. Clustering can be used for a variety of tasks, such as customer segmentation, image segmentation, and anomaly detection. Scikit-learn provides a comprehensive set of tools for clustering and evaluation, making it a great choice for many clustering tasks.

IV.II Dimensionality Reduction with Principal Component Analysis and t-SNE

Dimensionality reduction is an important technique in machine learning and data analysis that aims to reduce the number of features or variables in a dataset. This is often done to simplify data, remove noise, and make it easier to visualize and analyze. Two popular methods of dimensionality reduction are Principal Component Analysis (PCA) and t-Distributed Stochastic Neighbor Embedding (t-SNE).

In this section, we will learn how to use PCA and t-SNE for dimensionality reduction and visualization in Python using the scikit-learn library.

Installing Required Libraries

Before we start, let's make sure that we have the scikit-learn library installed. If it's not already installed, we can install it using pip:

```
$ pip install scikit-learn
```

We will also need the following libraries:

```
import numpy as np
import pandas as pd
import matplotlib.pyplot as plt
```

Loading and Preprocessing Data

To demonstrate the use of PCA and t-SNE, we will use the famous iris dataset. The dataset consists of 150 samples of iris flowers, each with four features: sepal length, sepal width, petal length, and petal width. The goal is to cluster the samples based on their features.

First, let's load the dataset using scikit-learn's datasets module:

```
from sklearn import datasets
iris = datasets.load_iris()
X = iris.data
y = iris.target
```

We can also normalize the data using scikit-learn's StandardScaler to scale the features so that each feature has a mean of 0 and a variance of 1:

```
from sklearn.preprocessing import StandardScaler
scaler = StandardScaler()
X_scaled = scaler.fit_transform(X)
```

Principal Component Analysis (PCA)

PCA is a linear dimensionality reduction technique that works by finding the principal components of a dataset, which are the directions of maximum variance. It then projects the data onto these principal components, reducing the number of dimensions.

To apply PCA to the iris dataset, we can use scikit-learn's PCA class:

```
from sklearn.decomposition import PCA
pca = PCA(n_components=2)
X_pca = pca.fit_transform(X_scaled)
```

We have set the number of components to 2, which means that we want to reduce the dimensionality of the dataset from 4 to 2.

We can now visualize the results of the PCA using a scatter plot:

```
plt.scatter(X_pca[:, 0], X_pca[:, 1], c=y)
```

```
plt.xlabel('First Principal Component')
plt.ylabel('Second Principal Component')
plt.show()
```

The scatter plot shows the reduced dataset with the target values (y) represented by different colors. We can see that the PCA has separated the samples into distinct clusters based on their features.

t-Distributed Stochastic Neighbor Embedding (t-SNE)

t-Distributed Stochastic Neighbor Embedding (t-SNE) is another popular dimensionality reduction technique used in machine learning. It is particularly useful for visualizing high-dimensional datasets. t-SNE maps the high-dimensional data points to a lower-dimensional space while preserving the pairwise similarities between the data points.

In scikit-learn, we can use the **TSNE** class from the **manifold** module to perform t-SNE. Here's an example:

```
from sklearn.manifold import TSNE
# Initialize t-SNE
tsne = TSNE(n_components=2, random_state=42)
# Perform t-SNE
X_tsne = tsne.fit_transform(X)
# Visualize the results
plt.scatter(X_tsne[:, 0], X_tsne[:, 1], c=y)
plt.show()
```

In this example, we initialized the **TSNE** class with **n_components=2** to reduce the data to 2 dimensions. We then fit and transformed the data using the **fit_transform** method, which returns the transformed data as a NumPy array. Finally, we visualized the results using a scatter plot, where the color of each point represents its class label.

t-SNE is computationally expensive and may not scale well to very large datasets. In such cases, other dimensionality reduction techniques such as PCA or truncated SVD may be more appropriate.

In summary, dimensionality reduction techniques such as PCA and t-SNE can be useful for visualizing and preprocessing high-dimensional datasets in machine learning. Scikit-learn provides several classes and functions for performing these techniques, making it easy to incorporate them into your machine-learning workflows.

V. DEEP LEARNING WITH TENSORFLOW AND KERAS

Deep learning has revolutionized the field of machine learning, enabling the creation of sophisticated models capable of learning from large and complex datasets. TensorFlow and Keras are two of the most popular libraries used for deep learning, providing a powerful and flexible platform for building and training deep neural networks. In this chapter, we will introduce the basics of deep learning and explore how to implement a variety of deep learning models using TensorFlow and Keras. We will cover topics such as artificial neural networks, convolutional neural networks, and recurrent neural networks, and demonstrate how to use these models for tasks such as image classification, natural language processing, and time series analysis. By the end of this chapter, you will have a solid foundation in deep learning and be equipped with the tools necessary to build your deep learning models.

V.I Introduction to Deep Learning

Deep learning is a subfield of machine learning that uses artificial neural networks to model and solve complex problems. Unlike traditional machine learning, which relies on feature engineering and domain expertise to create models, deep learning allows models to learn hierarchical representations of data directly from raw input. This makes it possible to build highly accurate and robust models for tasks such as image and speech recognition, natural language processing, and autonomous driving.

At the heart of deep learning are artificial neural networks, which are loosely inspired by the structure of the human brain. A neural network is composed of many interconnected processing nodes, or neurons, organized into layers. Each layer transforms the input data in some way, and the output of one layer serves as the input to the next. The first layer, known as the input layer, takes the raw data as input, and the final layer, known as the output layer, produces the final output of the network. In between the input and output layers, there may be one or more hidden layers, which are responsible for learning increasingly abstract representations of the input data.

To train a neural network, we must provide it with a set of labeled training examples. During training, the network learns to adjust the weights of its connections between neurons to minimize the difference between its predicted outputs and the true labels. This is typically done using an algorithm called backpropagation, which calculates the gradients of the network's error concerning its weights and uses these gradients to update the weights in the direction of lower error.

Deep learning has revolutionized the field of artificial intelligence and has led to breakthroughs in many areas, such as computer vision, speech recognition, and natural language processing. As the amount of available data continues to grow and the power of computing continues to increase, deep learning will likely continue to play a major role in shaping the future of AI.

V.II Introduction to TensorFlow and Keras

Deep learning has gained popularity in recent years, and TensorFlow and Keras are two popular libraries used in building and training deep learning models. TensorFlow is an open-source framework developed by Google for building and training machine learning models. Keras, on the other hand, is a high-level API built on top of TensorFlow, designed to simplify the process of building and training deep learning models.

In this section, we'll take a look at the basics of TensorFlow and Keras and explore some examples of how to use them to build deep learning models.

TensorFlow

TensorFlow is an open-source machine learning framework developed by the Google Brain team. It was designed to be an end-to-end platform for building and deploying machine learning models. TensorFlow provides a set of tools and APIs for building and training deep learning models, including neural networks.

One of the key features of TensorFlow is its ability to handle large datasets, making it ideal for deep learning applications. TensorFlow also provides a range of pre-built models, allowing users to easily build and train models for a variety of tasks.

Installing TensorFlow

To use TensorFlow, you need to install it on your machine. You can install TensorFlow using pip, a package manager for Python. Here's the command to install TensorFlow:

```
$ pip install tensorflow
```

Once you've installed TensorFlow, you can start building and training models.

Building a Simple Model in TensorFlow

To build a simple model in TensorFlow, you need to create a computational graph. A computational graph is a set of operations that are executed in a specific order to produce a result. The graph consists of nodes and edges, where the nodes represent the operations and the edges represent the data that flows between the nodes.

Here's an example of how to build a simple computational graph in TensorFlow:

```python
import tensorflow as tf
# Create a placeholder for the input data
x = tf.placeholder(tf.float32, [None, 2])
# Create a weight matrix and a bias vector
W = tf.Variable(tf.zeros([2, 1]))
b = tf.Variable(tf.zeros([1]))
# Define the output of the model
y = tf.matmul(x, W) + b
# Initialize the variables
init = tf.global_variables_initializer()
# Create a session and run the graph
with tf.Session() as sess:
    sess.run(init)
    result = sess.run(y, feed_dict={x: [[1, 2], [2, 3], [3, 4]]})
    print(result)
```

In this example, we're building a simple linear regression model. The model takes a two-dimensional input and produces a one-dimensional output. We start by creating a placeholder for the input data, which is a two-dimensional matrix. We then create a weight matrix and a bias vector, which are the parameters of the model. We define the output of the model as the matrix multiplication of the input data and the weight matrix, plus the bias vector. Finally, we initialize the variables and run the graph in a session.

TensorFlow APIs

TensorFlow provides a range of APIs for building and training deep learning models. Some of the most commonly used APIs include:

- **tf.nn**: a module for building neural networks.
- **tf.layers**: a module for building layers in a neural network.
- **tf.losses**: a module for defining loss functions.
- **tf.train**: a module for training models.

These APIs provide a range of tools for building and training models, including tools for handling data, defining layers, and optimizing models.

Keras

Keras is a high-level neural network API written in Python, which is built on top of TensorFlow. It provides a user-friendly interface for building deep learning models, allowing developers to focus on the design of the neural network rather than the low-level details of the underlying hardware and software.

Keras supports both convolutional neural networks (CNNs) and recurrent neural networks (RNNs), as well as combinations of the two. It also includes a wide range of pre-built layers, activation functions, and loss functions, making it easy to build and train neural networks for a variety of tasks.

One of the strengths of Keras is its flexibility. It can run on top of TensorFlow, Microsoft Cognitive Toolkit, Theano, or PlaidML. Keras can also be used with GPUs and TPUs for fast training and supports distributed training across multiple machines.

In the next sections, we will dive deeper into the Keras API, starting with the basics of building and training a neural network.

V.III Building Neural Networks with Keras

Keras is a high-level neural networks API, written in Python and capable of running on top of TensorFlow, CNTK, or Theano. It was developed with a focus on enabling fast experimentation and prototyping of deep learning models. In this section, we'll go over the basics of building neural networks with Keras.

Installing Keras

Before we get started, you'll need to install Keras. You can do this via pip:

`$ pip install keras`

Alternatively, if you're using Anaconda, you can install Keras using conda:

`$ conda install keras`

Understanding Neural Networks

A neural network is a series of interconnected layers, where each layer consists of multiple artificial neurons, also known as nodes. These nodes are connected via weights, and they process input data to produce an output.

The main components of a neural network are:

- Input layer: This layer receives input data.
- Hidden layers: These layers process the input data and perform transformations.
- Output layer: This layer produces the final output.

Building a Simple Neural Network

Let's start by building a simple neural network that can classify handwritten digits from the MNIST dataset. We'll use a fully connected network with two hidden layers.

```python
import keras
from keras.datasets import mnist
from keras.models import Sequential
from keras.layers import Dense, Dropout
from keras.optimizers import RMSprop
# Load the MNIST dataset
(x_train, y_train), (x_test, y_test) = mnist.load_data()
# Preprocess the data
x_train = x_train.reshape(60000, 784)
x_test = x_test.reshape(10000, 784)
x_train = x_train.astype('float32')
x_test = x_test.astype('float32')
x_train /= 255
x_test /= 255
y_train = keras.utils.to_categorical(y_train, 10)
y_test = keras.utils.to_categorical(y_test, 10)
# Build the model
model = Sequential()
model.add(Dense(512, activation='relu', input_shape=(784,)))
model.add(Dropout(0.2))
model.add(Dense(512, activation='relu'))
model.add(Dropout(0.2))
model.add(Dense(10, activation='softmax'))
```

```python
# Compile the model
model.compile(loss='categorical_crossentropy',
        optimizer=RMSprop(),
        metrics=['accuracy'])
# Train the model
history = model.fit(x_train, y_train,
            batch_size=128,
            epochs=20,
            verbose=1,
            validation_data=(x_test, y_test))
# Evaluate the model
score = model.evaluate(x_test, y_test, verbose=0)
print('Test loss:', score[0])
print('Test accuracy:', score[1])
```

Let's go over the code step by step:

1. We import the necessary modules from Keras.

2. We load the MNIST dataset and preprocess the data. The images are reshaped to 784-dimensional vectors and normalized to have values between 0 and 1. The labels are one-hot encoded.

3. We define the architecture of the neural network. The first two layers are fully connected layers with 512 units and ReLU activation. We also apply dropout regularization to prevent overfitting. The final layer is a fully connected layer with 10 units and softmax activation, which outputs the probability distribution over the 10 classes.

4. We compile the model by specifying the loss function, optimizer, and evaluation metric.

5. We train the model on the training set for 20 epochs with a batch size of 128.

6. We evaluate the model on the test set and print the test loss and accuracy.

Saving and Loading Models

Once you've trained a model, you may want to save it for later use. You can save a Keras model to a file using the save method:

```
model.save('model.h5')
```

This will save the entire model (architecture, weights, and optimizer state) to a single HDF5 file.

To load a saved model, you can use the load_model function:

```
from keras.models import load_model
model = load_model('model.h5')
```

Conclusion

In this section, we went over the basics of building neural networks with Keras. We built a simple fully connected network for classifying handwritten digits from the MNIST dataset, and we learned how to save and load models. Keras offers many more types of layers, activation functions, loss functions, and optimization algorithms, so feel free to experiment with different configurations to see what works best for your problem. Happy coding!

Another Example

1. Building a Simple Neural Network

Let's build a simple neural network for a classification problem using Keras. We will use the Sequential model and add layers to it.

```
import tensorflow as tf
from tensorflow.keras import layers
# Define the model
model = tf.keras.Sequential()
# Add input layer
model.add(layers.Dense(units=128,          activation='relu',
input_shape=(784,)))
# Add hidden layers
model.add(layers.Dense(units=64, activation='relu'))
model.add(layers.Dense(units=32, activation='relu'))
# Add output layer
model.add(layers.Dense(units=10, activation='softmax'))
# Display the model summary
model.summary()
```

In this example, we have an input layer with 784 nodes, two hidden layers with 64 and 32 nodes, and an output layer with 10 nodes. The activation functions used are ReLU for the input and hidden layers, and softmax for the output layer.

2. Compiling the Model

Before training, we need to compile the model. We'll specify the optimizer, loss function, and evaluation metrics.

```
model.compile(optimizer='adam',
loss='sparse_categorical_crossentropy', metrics=['accuracy'])
```

In this example, we use the Adam optimizer and sparse categorical crossentropy as the loss function, as it's a multi-class classification problem. We also track the accuracy metric.

3. Training the Model

To train the model, we need to provide input data and corresponding labels. We'll use the famous MNIST dataset of handwritten digits for this example. Keras includes a utility function to load the dataset.

```
# Load the data
(x_train,        y_train),        (x_test,        y_test)        =
tf.keras.datasets.mnist.load_data()
# Preprocess the data
x_train = x_train.reshape(-1, 784) / 255.0
x_test = x_test.reshape(-1, 784) / 255.0
# Train the model
history = model.fit(x_train, y_train, epochs=10, batch_size=32,
validation_split=0.2)
```

We reshape the input data to be a flat array of 784 elements (28x28 pixels), and normalize the pixel values between 0 and 1. We then train the model using the fit() method with a batch size of 32 and 10 epochs. We also set aside 20% of the training data for validation.

4. Evaluating the Model

To evaluate the model's performance, we can use the evaluate() method with the test data.

```
loss, accuracy = model.evaluate(x_test, y_test)
print("Test Loss:", loss)
print("Test Accuracy:", accuracy)
```

Conclusion

In this section, we learned how to build, compile, train, and evaluate a simple neural network using Keras. Keras makes it easy to create and experiment with different network architectures, and it's a powerful tool for deep learning practitioners.

V.IV Convolutional Neural Networks for Image Classification

Convolutional Neural Networks (CNNs) are a powerful class of neural networks that are particularly well-suited for image classification tasks. In this section, we'll go over the basics of building CNNs for image classification using Keras.

Installing Keras and TensorFlow

Before we get started, you'll need to install Keras and TensorFlow. You can do this via pip:

```
$ pip install keras tensorflow
```

Alternatively, if you're using Anaconda, you can install Keras and TensorFlow using conda:

```
$ conda install keras tensorflow
```

Building a Simple CNN

Let's start by building a simple CNN for classifying images from the CIFAR-10 dataset. We'll use a small CNN with two convolutional layers and two fully connected layers.

```
import keras

from keras.datasets import cifar10

from keras.models import Sequential

from keras.layers import Dense, Dropout, Flatten, Conv2D, MaxPooling2D

# Load the CIFAR-10 dataset

(x_train, y_train), (x_test, y_test) = cifar10.load_data()

# Preprocess the data
```

```python
x_train = x_train.astype('float32')
x_test = x_test.astype('float32')
x_train /= 255
x_test /= 255
y_train = keras.utils.to_categorical(y_train, 10)
y_test = keras.utils.to_categorical(y_test, 10)
# Build the model
model = Sequential()
model.add(Conv2D(32, (3, 3), padding='same', activation='relu',
input_shape=x_train.shape[1:]))
model.add(Conv2D(32, (3, 3), activation='relu'))
model.add(MaxPooling2D(pool_size=(2, 2)))
model.add(Dropout(0.25))
model.add(Conv2D(64, (3, 3), padding='same', activation='relu'))
model.add(Conv2D(64, (3, 3), activation='relu'))
model.add(MaxPooling2D(pool_size=(2, 2)))
model.add(Dropout(0.25))
model.add(Flatten())
model.add(Dense(512, activation='relu'))
model.add(Dropout(0.5))
model.add(Dense(10, activation='softmax'))
# Compile the model
model.compile(loss='categorical_crossentropy',
        optimizer='adam',
        metrics=['accuracy'])
# Train the model
history = model.fit(x_train, y_train,
```

```
            batch_size=128,
            epochs=20,
            verbose=1,
            validation_data=(x_test, y_test))
# Evaluate the model
score = model.evaluate(x_test, y_test, verbose=0)
print('Test loss:', score[0])
print('Test accuracy:', score[1])
```

Let's go over the code step by step:

1. We import the necessary modules from Keras.

2. We load the CIFAR-10 dataset and preprocess the data. The images are normalized to have values between 0 and 1, and the labels are one-hot encoded.

3. We define the architecture of the CNN. The first layer is a convolutional layer with 32 filters, each of size 3x3, and ReLU activation. The second layer is another convolutional layer with 32 filters, each of size 3x3, and ReLU activation, followed by max pooling and dropout regularization. The third and fourth layers are similar to the first two, but with 64 filters instead of 32. The fifth layer is a fully connected layer with 512 units and ReLU activation, followed by dropout regularization. The final layer is a fully connected layer with 10 units and softmax activation, which outputs the probability distribution over the 10 classes.

4. We compile the model by specifying the loss function, optimizer, and evaluation metric.

5. We train the model on the training set for 20 epochs with a batch size of 128.

6. We evaluate the model on the test set and print the test

loss and accuracy.

Visualizing Filters

One of the advantages of CNNs is that the filters in the convolutional layers can be visualized to gain insight into what the network is learning. Let's visualize the filters in the first convolutional layer of our CNN.

```python
import matplotlib.pyplot as plt
# Get the weights of the first convolutional layer
filters, biases = model.layers[0].get_weights()
# Rescale the filters to be between 0 and 1
f_min, f_max = filters.min(), filters.max()
filters = (filters - f_min) / (f_max - f_min)
# Plot the filters
n_filters, ix = 6, 1
for i in range(n_filters):
  for j in range(n_filters):
    # Get the filter
    filter = filters[:, :, :, ix]
# Plot each channel separately
for k in range(3):
ax = plt.subplot(n_filters, n_filters, ix)
ax.set_xticks([])
ax.set_yticks([])
plt.imshow(filter[:, :, k], cmap='gray')
ix += 1
```

Show the plot

```python
plt.show()
```

This code will plot each of the 32 filters in the first convolutional layer as a 3x3 grid of grayscale images.

Conclusion

In this section, we went over the basics of building CNNs for image classification using Keras. We built a small CNN for classifying images from the CIFAR-10 dataset, and we learned how to visualize the filters in the convolutional layers. There are many ways to modify and extend CNNs, so feel free to experiment with different architectures and hyperparameters to see what works best for your problem. Happy coding!

V.V Recurrent Neural Networks
for Text Classification

Recurrent Neural Networks (RNNs) are a powerful class of neural networks that are particularly well-suited for processing sequential data, such as text. In this section, we'll go over the basics of building RNNs for text classification using Keras.

Installing Keras and TensorFlow

Before we get started, you'll need to install Keras and TensorFlow. You can do this via pip:

```
$ pip install keras tensorflow
```

Alternatively, if you're using Anaconda, you can install Keras and TensorFlow using conda:

```
$ conda install keras tensorflow
```

Building a Simple RNN

Let's start by building a simple RNN for classifying movie reviews as positive or negative. We'll use the IMDB dataset, which consists of 50,000 movie reviews with binary sentiment labels.

```
import keras
from keras.datasets import imdb
from keras.models import Sequential
from keras.layers import Dense, Dropout, LSTM, Embedding
from keras.preprocessing import sequence
# Load the IMDB dataset
```

```python
(x_train, y_train), (x_test, y_test) = imdb.load_data(num_words=10000)
# Pad the sequences to the same length
max_review_length = 500
x_train = sequence.pad_sequences(x_train, maxlen=max_review_length)
x_test = sequence.pad_sequences(x_test, maxlen=max_review_length)
# Build the model
model = Sequential()
model.add(Embedding(10000, 32, input_length=max_review_length))
model.add(LSTM(100))
model.add(Dense(1, activation='sigmoid'))
# Compile the model
model.compile(loss='binary_crossentropy',
       optimizer='adam',
       metrics=['accuracy'])
# Train the model
history = model.fit(x_train, y_train,
        batch_size=64,
        epochs=10,
        verbose=1,
        validation_data=(x_test, y_test))
# Evaluate the model
score = model.evaluate(x_test, y_test, verbose=0)
print('Test loss:', score[0])
print('Test accuracy:', score[1])
```

Let's go over the code step by step:

1. We import the necessary modules from Keras.

2. We load the IMDB dataset and preprocess the data. We keep only the 10,000 most frequent words and pad the sequences to a fixed length of 500.

3. We define the architecture of the RNN. The first layer is an embedding layer, which maps each word to a 32-dimensional vector. The second layer is an LSTM layer with 100 units. The final layer is a fully connected layer with 1 unit and sigmoid activation, which outputs the probability of the review being positive.

4. We compile the model by specifying the loss function, optimizer, and evaluation metric.

5. We train the model on the training set for 10 epochs with a batch size of 64.

6. We evaluate the model on the test set and print the test loss and accuracy.

Visualizing Attention

One of the advantages of RNNs is that they can be used to visualize attention over the input sequence, which can help to understand what parts of the sequence are most important for the classification. Let's visualize the attention over the input sequence for a few example reviews.

```
import numpy as np
import matplotlib.pyplot as plt
# Get the attention weights for the LSTM layer
attention_layer = model.layers[1]
weights = attention_layer.get_weights()[0]
# Get the word index to word mapping for the IMDB dataset
```

```
word_index = imdb.get_word_index()

reverse_word_index = dict([(value, key) for (key, value) in word_index.items()])

decoded_review = ' '.join([reverse_word_index.get(i - 3, '?') for i in x_test[0]])

# Compute the attention weights for the first review

attention_weights = np.dot(weights, np.transpose(x_test[0]))

# Plot the attention weights for the first review

plt.figure(figsize=(16, 8))

plt.bar(range(len(decoded_review.split())),
attention_weights[:len(decoded_review.split())])

plt.xticks(range(len(decoded_review.split())),
decoded_review.split(), rotation=90)

plt.show()
```

This code will compute the attention weights for the first review in the test set and plot them as a bar chart over the words in the review.

Conclusion

In this section, we went over the basics of building RNNs for text classification using Keras. We built a simple RNN for classifying movie reviews as positive or negative, and we learned how to visualize the attention over the input sequence. There are many ways to modify and extend RNNs, so feel free to experiment with different architectures and hyperparameters to see what works best for your problem. Happy coding!

VI. CASE STUDIES

D
ata science and machine learning have become essential tools for businesses looking to gain insights, optimize operations, and improve decision-making. In this chapter, we will explore several case studies where data science and machine learning were used to solve real-world problems, ranging from customer churn prediction to predictive maintenance. Through these case studies, we will see how data science and machine learning can provide valuable solutions to complex business challenges, and how they continue to transform the way businesses operate.

VI.I Applying the learned techniques to real-world problems

Data Science and Machine Learning have become ubiquitous in today's world, and many businesses are adopting these technologies to gain insights and improve their operations. In this section, we will explore some case studies where data science and machine learning have been used to solve real-world problems.

Case Study 1: Predicting Customer Churn

One of the biggest challenges for businesses is retaining customers. In the telecommunications industry, for example, customer churn is a major problem. A telecommunications company approached a data science consulting firm to help them predict which customers were likely to churn so that they could take proactive measures to retain them.

The data science team used machine learning algorithms to analyze customer data, such as usage patterns, billing history, and customer demographics. They developed a predictive model that could identify customers who were at high risk of churning, and the company used this model to target these customers with special offers and promotions. As a result, the company was able to reduce customer churn by 15%, which translated into significant cost savings and increased revenue.

Case Study 2: Fraud Detection

Fraud is a major problem for financial institutions, and detecting fraudulent transactions can be a difficult and time-consuming process. A large bank approached a data science consulting firm to help them develop a machine learning model that could identify fraudulent transactions in real time.

The data science team used a combination of supervised and unsupervised learning algorithms to analyze transaction data, such as transaction amount, merchant location, and customer history. They developed a predictive model that could identify fraudulent transactions with high accuracy, and the bank integrated this model into their transaction processing system. As a result, the bank was able to identify and prevent fraudulent transactions in real time, which saved them millions of dollars in losses.

Case Study 3: Predictive Maintenance

Predictive maintenance is the practice of using data analytics to predict when equipment is likely to fail so that maintenance can be scheduled proactively. A manufacturing company approached a data science consulting firm to help them implement a predictive maintenance program for their machinery.

The data science team used machine learning algorithms to analyze sensor data from the machinery, such as temperature, pressure, and vibration. They developed a predictive model that could identify when the machinery was likely to fail, and the company used this model to schedule maintenance proactively. As a result, the company was able to reduce downtime and maintenance costs, which improved its overall efficiency and profitability.

Conclusion

Data science and machine learning have revolutionized the way businesses operate, by providing insights and solutions to complex problems. In this section, we explored three case studies where data science and machine learning were used to predict customer churn, detect fraud, and implement predictive maintenance. These are just a few examples of the many ways in which data science and machine learning are being used to drive business value. As these technologies continue to evolve, we can expect to see even more innovative use cases in the future.

VI.II Examples of data science and machine learning projects

Data Science and Machine Learning are rapidly growing fields that have the potential to revolutionize the way we approach problems and make decisions. In this section, we will explore some examples of Data Science and Machine Learning projects that have been undertaken in various domains and industries, to showcase the wide range of applications of these technologies.

Example 1: Predicting Energy Consumption

One of the biggest challenges for energy providers is predicting the demand for energy, which can vary significantly over time. A Data Science team at a power utility company developed a machine learning model to predict energy consumption based on historical data, weather forecasts, and other factors. The model was able to accurately predict energy consumption, which allowed the company to optimize its energy production and reduce costs.

Example 2: Fraud Detection in Banking

Fraud detection is a major concern for banks and financial institutions. A team of Data Scientists at a large bank developed a machine-learning model to detect fraudulent transactions in real time. The model analyzed transaction data, such as transaction amount, merchant location, and customer history, and was able to identify fraudulent transactions with high accuracy. This allowed the bank to prevent fraud before it occurred, which saved them millions of dollars in losses.

Example 3: Improving Healthcare Outcomes

Healthcare is an area where Data Science and Machine Learning can have a significant impact. A team of Data Scientists at a hospital developed a machine-learning model to predict which patients were likely to be readmitted after being discharged. The model analyzed patient data, such as medical history, lab results, and demographic information, and was able to accurately predict readmissions. This allowed the hospital to intervene early and provide targeted care to high-risk patients, which improved healthcare outcomes and reduced costs.

Example 4: Recommender System for E-commerce

Recommender systems are a popular application of Data Science and Machine Learning in the e-commerce domain. A team of Data Scientists at an online retailer developed a recommender system to suggest products to customers based on their browsing and purchase history. The system used collaborative filtering algorithms to identify similar customers and recommend products that they had purchased. This led to increased sales and customer satisfaction, as customers were more likely to purchase products that were relevant to their interests.

Example 5: Natural language processing in customer service

Natural language processing (NLP) is a field of artificial intelligence that deals with the interaction between computers and human languages. NLP can be used in customer service to analyze customer feedback and respond to customer inquiries. For example, chatbots powered by NLP can respond to customer inquiries in real time, improving customer service and reducing response times. Companies like Airbnb and Uber use chatbots to assist with customer inquiries and support.

Conclusion

In this section, we explored some examples of Data Science and Machine Learning projects across various domains and industries. These projects showcase the wide range of applications of these technologies, from predicting energy consumption to improving healthcare outcomes. As Data Science and Machine Learning continue to evolve, we can expect to see even more innovative and impactful projects in the future.

VII. CONCLUSION

In conclusion, Python is a powerful and flexible programming language that has become the go-to choice for data science and machine learning projects. With the tools and techniques covered in this book, you should now be equipped with the essential knowledge and skills to start working with data in Python.

From data cleaning and preprocessing to data visualization and modeling, you have learned about the fundamental concepts and practical applications of various Python libraries, including NumPy, Pandas, Matplotlib, Scikit-learn, and Keras. Whether you are interested in data analysis, predictive modeling, or deep learning, these libraries provide a solid foundation for building robust and scalable data-driven solutions.

Remember, mastering data science and machine learning is an ongoing process, and it requires continuous learning and practice. As you continue to work with data, you will encounter new challenges and opportunities to apply your skills and knowledge. However, with the foundational knowledge and practical experience gained from this book, you are well on your way to becoming a proficient data scientist or machine learning engineer.

I hope this book has been a helpful resource in your journey to mastering data science and machine learning in Python. Good luck and happy coding!

VII.I Recap of the most important concepts

Chapter I: Getting started with Python and its Data Science Libraries

- Data science involves using data to make informed decisions or predictions
- Python is a popular programming language for data science
- Python has a large ecosystem of libraries and tools for data manipulation, analysis, and visualization

Chapter II: Working with Data in Python

- Data can be loaded into Python using libraries like NumPy, Pandas, and Matplotlib
- Data cleaning and manipulation can be done using Pandas
- Categorical data can be encoded using one-hot encoding or label encoding
- Data scaling and normalization can improve the performance of machine learning algorithms
- Feature engineering can improve the quality of the data and lead to better machine-learning models
- Data visualization can help to understand the data and communicate insights

Chapter III: Supervised Learning with Scikit-learn

- Scikit-learn is a popular machine-learning library for Python
- Linear regression can be used to model the relationship between a dependent variable and one or more

independent variables

- Logistic regression can be used for binary classification problems

- Decision trees and random forests can be used for classification and regression problems

- Support vector machines can be used for classification and regression problems

- K-nearest neighbors can be used for classification and regression problems

- Naive Bayes can be used for classification problems

- Model evaluation and metrics can be used to evaluate the performance of machine learning models

Chapter IV: Unsupervised Learning with Scikit-learn

- Unsupervised learning involves finding patterns in data without a specific outcome in mind

- Clustering algorithms like K-means and hierarchical clustering can be used to group similar data points together

- Dimensionality reduction techniques like principal component analysis (PCA) and t-SNE can be used to visualize high-dimensional data

Chapter V: Deep Learning with TensorFlow and Keras

- Deep learning involves training neural networks with multiple layers

- TensorFlow and Keras are popular libraries for building and training deep-learning models

- Neural networks can be used for classification and regression problems

- Convolutional neural networks can be used for image

classification problems

- Recurrent neural networks can be used for sequence prediction problems

These are just some of the most important concepts covered in the book. By mastering these concepts and techniques, you'll be well on your way to becoming a proficient data scientist and machine learning practitioner.

VII.II Future directions in data science and machine learning

The field of data science and machine learning is constantly evolving and advancing. Here are some exciting directions that the field is moving towards:

1. **Deep learning and neural networks:** Deep learning has already had a significant impact on the field of artificial intelligence and machine learning. In the future, we can expect to see more sophisticated neural networks and architectures that can handle increasingly complex tasks.

2. **Reinforcement learning:** Reinforcement learning is a type of machine learning that involves an agent learning to interact with an environment to maximize some kind of reward. It has shown promising results in a variety of domains, including game-playing, robotics, and autonomous driving.

3. **Natural language processing:** Natural language processing (NLP) is a branch of artificial intelligence that focuses on understanding and generating human language. NLP has already had a significant impact on the field of data science, and we can expect to see further advances in this area in the future, including improved language models and better text-to-speech technology.

4. **Explainable AI:** As machine learning models become more complex, it is becoming increasingly important to understand how they make decisions. Explainable AI aims to provide insights into how machine learning models work, allowing us to better understand and interpret their results.

5. **Edge computing:** Edge computing involves running machine learning models on devices at the edge of a network, such as smartphones or IoT devices, rather than in the cloud. This can provide faster and more efficient processing and has the potential to enable new types of applications and use cases.

These are just a few of the many exciting directions that the field of data science and machine learning is moving towards. As new tools and techniques are developed, we can expect to see even more innovative applications of these technologies in a wide range of industries and domains.

VII.III Additional resources
for further learning

Here are some additional resources for further learning on the topics covered in this book:

1. **Pandas Documentation:** The official documentation for Pandas, provides a comprehensive guide to all the features and functionalities of the library. Available at https://pandas.pydata.org/docs/.

2. **NumPy Documentation:** The official documentation for NumPy, provides a comprehensive guide to all the features and functionalities of the library. Available at https://numpy.org/doc/.

3. **Matplotlib Documentation:** The official documentation for Matplotlib, provides a comprehensive guide to all the features and functionalities of the library. Available at https:// matplotlib.org/stable/contents.html.

4. **Scikit-learn Documentation:** The official documentation for Scikit-learn, provides a comprehensive guide to all the features and functionalities of the library. Available at https:// scikit-learn.org/stable/documentation.html.

5. **TensorFlow Documentation:** The official documentation for TensorFlow, provides a comprehensive guide to all the features and functionalities of the library. Available at https:// www.tensorflow.org/api_docs/python.

6. **Keras Documentation:** The official documentation for Keras, provides a comprehensive guide to all the features and functionalities of the library. Available at https://keras.io/api/.

7. **Kaggle:** A platform for data science competitions and projects, where users can work with real-world datasets and compete against other data scientists. Available at https://www.kaggle.com/.

8. **Towards Data Science:** A popular publication and community for data science enthusiasts, featuring articles and sections on a wide range of topics in data science and machine learning. Available at https://towardsdatascience.com/.

These resources can help you continue your learning and exploration of the exciting field of data science and machine learning.

EPILOGUE

Congratulations on completing "Python for Data Science and Machine Learning: Essential Tools for Working with Data"! By now, you should have a solid foundation in the fundamentals of Python programming, data science, and machine learning. But the journey doesn't end here.

The field of data science and machine learning is constantly evolving, with new tools, techniques, and applications emerging every day. As you continue your learning journey, here are some tips to help you stay up-to-date and take your skills to the next level:

1. Join a community: The data science and machine learning community is a vibrant and supportive group of professionals and enthusiasts. Join online forums, attend meetups, and participate in online courses to connect with others and learn from their experiences.
2. Read blogs and research papers: There are countless blogs and research papers on data science and machine learning, with new ones being published every day. Follow thought leaders and stay up-to-date on the latest developments in the field.
3. Experiment with new tools and techniques: Don't be afraid to try new tools and techniques. Experiment with different

libraries, algorithms, and approaches to see what works best for your specific use case.

4. Work on real-world projects: The best way to solidify your skills is to apply them to real-world projects. Look for opportunities to work on data science and machine learning projects, whether it's through a job, freelance work, or personal projects.

5. Keep learning: Learning is a lifelong process, and there is always more to discover in data science and machine learning. Whether it's through books, courses, or practical experience, keep pushing yourself to learn more and improve your skills.

Thank you for choosing "Python for Data Science and Machine Learning: Essential Tools for Working with Data" as your learning resource. I hope it has provided you with a solid foundation and inspiration to continue your learning journey. Best of luck in all your future endeavors!

ABOUT THE AUTHOR

Moustafa Elgezery

As a Linux expert, data scientist, machine learning engineer, and author, I'm passionate about using technology to solve complex problems and drive innovation. With over ten years of experience in the industry, I have honed my skills in areas such as Linux administration, IT automation, Scripting, Data preprocessing, and analysis, interpreting data to help drive decision-making, and researching,  building, and designing self-running artificial intelligence (AI) systems to automate predictive models.

I prioritize integrity, excellence, innovation, collaboration, and impact. I strive to stay up-to-date with the latest developments in my field.

As an author, I believe sharing knowledge is crucial to advancing this field and enabling others to succeed. I dedicate myself to using my skills and expertise to achieve a positive impact worldwide, and I am excited to continue growing and learning in my work.

BOOKS BY THIS AUTHOR

Artificial Intelligence (Ai) In Business: Real-World Case Studies And Applications

Unlock the potential of AI for your business with 'Artificial Intelligence (AI) in Business: Real-World Case Studies and Applications'. This comprehensive guide offers a deep dive into the latest trends, tools, and techniques driving AI innovation in today's business world.

Explore a wealth of real-world case studies and practical applications from top companies across industries, revealing how AI can transform operations, drive revenue growth, and optimize decision-making. From predictive analytics and natural language processing to computer vision and deep learning, gain a comprehensive understanding of the different AI technologies and their respective business use cases.

Written in an engaging and accessible style, this book is a must-read for anyone looking to harness the power of AI to drive business success. Whether you're a seasoned professional or new to the field, 'Artificial Intelligence (AI) in Business' offers a wealth of insights and best practices to help you stay ahead of the curve and achieve your goals.

THANK YOU!